AIM Higher!

New York ELA Review

Level D

Robert D. Shepherd

Victoria S. Fortune

aim higher!®

Great Source Education Group
A division of Houghton Mifflin Company
Wilmington, MA

www.greatsource.com

Editorial Staff

Dan Carsen
Diane Perkins Castro
Victoria S. Fortune
Barbara R. Stratton

Design & Production

Paige Larkin

Cover Design

Seann Dwyer, Studio Montage, St. Louis

Cover Photo

© Jim Cummins/CORBIS

Consultant

Victor Jaccarino
  English Department Chairperson, Herricks High School
  Hyde Park, NY

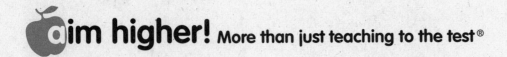

Second Edition

Printed in the United States of America

2 3 4 5 6 7 8 9 10   DBH   10 09 08

International Standard Book Number-13: 978-1-58171-718-1
International Standard Book Number-10: 1-58171-718-0

Contents

Pretest 1

Unit 1 • Test-Taking Strategies 37

First Encounter "Campfire Stories" 38

Chapter 1 This Is Only a Test • Taking Tests 44
Understanding Test Questions 44
Answering Written-Response Questions 46
Getting Ready to Take a Test 51

Chapter 2 On Closer Examination • Understanding Your State Test 53
What to Expect on the ELA Exam 54
How the ELA Exam Is Divided Up 55
How the ELA Exam Is Scored 55

Unit 2 • Reading Skills Review 57

First Encounter "Dogs for Work, Play, and Show" 58

Chapter 3 Talking Back to Books • Active Reading 65
Before Reading: Previewing a Passage 65
During Reading: Active Reading Strategies 69
During Reading: Dealing with Difficult Vocabulary 75
Word Parts 77
After Reading: Reflecting and Responding 85

Chapter 4 I Think I've Got It! • Reading Comprehension 87
Find the Main Idea 88
Figure Out the Sequence 93
Look for Causes and Effects 96
Look for Context Clues 100
Find the Theme 104

Unit 3 • A World of Good Reading 109

First Encounter "Mr. Handyman," "Thanks to Dad" 110

Chapter 5 Truth Be Told • Understanding Nonfiction 116
              What Is Nonfiction? 116
              Types of Informative Nonfiction 124
              Narrative Nonfiction 129

Chapter 6 A Tale to Tell • Understanding Fiction 134
              What Is Fiction? 134
              Analyzing Fiction 135

Chapter 7 Words That Sing • Understanding Poetry 138
              What Is Poetry? 138
              The Sounds of Poetry 138
              Meaning in Poetry 145

Unit 4 • Listening, Notetaking, and Graphic Organizers 147

First Encounter "From Slave to Civil Rights Leader" 148

Chapter 8 Hold That Thought • Introduction to Notetaking 152
              What Are Notes? 152
              When to Take Notes 152
              How to Take Notes 153

Chapter 9 Picture This! • Taking Notes with Graphic Organizers 159
              Using Word Webs 159
              Using Charts 160
              Other Graphic Organizers 161

Chapter 10 Listen Up! • Listening and Taking Notes 166
              Active Listening 166
              Listening and Taking Notes on Stories 167
              Listening and Taking Notes on Nonfiction 168

Unit 5 • Writing Skills Review 175

First Encounter "A Letter to a Pen Pal" 177

Chapter 11   Step by Step • The Writing Process 179
                 Prewriting 181
                 Drafting 192
                 Evaluating and Revising 195
                 Proofreading 199
                 Publishing or Sharing 203

Chapter 12   Sentence Sense • Building Strong Sentences 205
                 Writing Complete Sentences 205
                 Using a Variety of Sentence Types 207
                 Combining and Expanding Sentences 213
                 Reviewing Your Writing 219

Chapter 13   Perfect Paragraphs • Main Ideas and Supporting Details 222
                 What Is a Paragraph? 222
                 Sample Writing Prompt and Answer 225

Chapter 14   Excellent Essays • Introduction, Body, and Conclusion 229
                 Writing the Introduction 231
                 Writing the Body of the Essay 234
                 Writing the Conclusion 236

Posttest 241

Appendix A: Punctuation and Capitalization Handbook 277

Appendix B: "Student-Friendly" Writing Rubric 284

Glossary 285

Index 295

Pretest
English Language Arts

Session 1: Reading

In this part of the test, you are going to do some reading. Then you will answer questions about what you have read.

Session 1: Reading

Directions *Read this story. Then answer questions 1 through 5.*

The Story of the House: A Chinese Folktale

Long, long ago, there were mountains everywhere. People and wild animals and birds all lived together in caves. One day, the sky turned black. A fierce storm pounded the Earth. Rain came down very hard. The wind tore trees from the ground and threw big rocks around like pebbles. Mountains fell. Soon only three beings were left: a tiger, a dragon, and a young man.

They hid beneath a rock so heavy that the wind could not lift it, and so they were saved. As the water rose all around them, it flooded all the caves. Tiger, Dragon, and the young man could not return to their homes. They huddled together to keep warm.

"We must do something to stay alive," said the young man. "We must build a house."

"Yes, we must, and right away," said Tiger and Dragon in agreement. Tiger and Dragon rushed out and began looking for grass, twigs, and logs. The young man cut vines to use as ropes. Working hard, they soon built a warm, dry house.

For a while, they lived together in peace, but this did not last long. Tiger and Dragon both wanted the house for themselves. The three beings began to argue and fight. Things got so terrible that they all agreed they could not live together.

"Only one of us can stay in the house," said the young man.

GO ON

"Let's have a test. We will see which one of us can drive the other two out of the house," Tiger said. "The one who wins can keep the house!"

Dragon and the young man agreed.

"I'll try first," Tiger roared. "I'll get you two out!"

Tiger leaped out of the house. He ripped up grass and trees and roared. The young man and Dragon huddled together in a corner as trees and rocks flew and the house shook. They were frightened, but they did not run outside.

Tiger soon got tired and came back into the house.

"Now I'll try," said Dragon as he left the house.

Dragon roared and let loose thunder, lightning, and hail. He created a great rain and a howling wind. The sound was awful. Tiger and the young man clung to each other in fright, but they did not leave the house. Tired and angry, Dragon came back in.

"Now it's my turn," said the young man, and he walked out the door.

He rubbed two stones together to make a small flame. Then he lit the dry grass on the roof on fire. As the grass burned, smoke blew into the house. Tiger and Dragon sniffed. They heard the crackling of the fire. In the blink of an eye, they ran outside.

Tiger ran into the forest, and Dragon ran to the sea. The young man put out his fire. Then he went into his house.

Tiger liked the forest. Dragon liked the sea. The young man liked his house. And there they have stayed ever since, each in his own home, free from the others. ○

1. Which sentence BEST tells what this story is about?
   - Ⓐ A young man, a dragon, and a tiger have to decide who gets to live in the house.
   - Ⓑ A young man, a dragon, and a tiger survive a storm and become great friends.
   - Ⓒ A young man, a dragon, and a tiger build a houseboat and survive a terrible flood.
   - Ⓓ A young man, a dragon, and a tiger work together to defeat an evil giant.

2. After living together for a while, the tiger, the dragon, and the young man
   - Ⓐ finally become great friends.
   - Ⓑ begin to argue and fight.
   - Ⓒ learn how to work together.
   - Ⓓ all miss their families.

3. Read this sentence from the story:

   The young man and Dragon huddled together in a corner as trees and rocks flew and the house shook.

   Which of the following words has about the same meaning as *huddled*?
   - Ⓐ danced
   - Ⓑ stood
   - Ⓒ crouched
   - Ⓓ argued

4. How does the dragon try to make the others leave the house?
   - Ⓐ He throws trees and rocks around and makes the house shake.
   - Ⓑ He creates a terrible storm with thunder, lightning, and hail.
   - Ⓒ He creates a fierce rainstorm that floods the little house.
   - Ⓓ He sets the roof of the house on fire and smokes them out.

5. What happens as a result of the competition among the dragon, the tiger, and the young man?
   - Ⓐ The creatures become lifelong friends.
   - Ⓑ The creatures end up in the places that suit them best.
   - Ⓒ The young man becomes the ruler of the other creatures.
   - Ⓓ The creatures decide to live together.

Directions *Read this poem. Then answer questions 6 through 10.*

Max's Story
by Will Tripp

Max was a hound dog whose name was well known.
All the farmers around wished Max was their own.
For Max was quite fearsome, yet loyal and kind,
There was no better hound dog that you'd hope to find.

Max lived in the country on a nice little farm,
Where he made sure the animals came to no harm.
There were roosters, chickens, cows, pigs, and sheep,
And with Max nearby they could all safely sleep.

The coyotes and foxes found it quite hard
To sneak past Max when he was on guard.
His master, the farmer, said Max was like gold.
He'd say, "When they made Max, they broke the mold."

Max lived with another dog that was purebred,
She had pups "Oh, so cute," as everyone said.
The farmer planned for the pups to be bought.
"Who needs more dogs when there's Max?" he thought.

Everyone was happy; the dogs got along.
Max even helped the young pups to grow strong.
He knew that these pups would each find a home,
And the animals they guarded would be safe to roam.

Then late one night some trouble arose.
Max fell asleep and was not on his toes.
He was supposed to be watching the chickens that night
But while he was asleep they got quite a fright.

A fox had come by who was craving some meat.
He decided to stop for a quick bite to eat.
He snuck past Max, by the gate where he slept
And stealthily into the chicken coop crept.

When the fox got inside, he grinned with delight.
He was inside the coop with no Max in sight!
He darted at chickens, caught one in his jaws,
Then a bark sent the fox away on quick paws.

Max charged to the coop and saw what was done.
He felt so ashamed, for the sly fox had won.
Though no eggs were broken, the chickens were frantic;
Max saw one was gone and started to panic.

Old Max ran and hid in a field of grain,
Till he heard his master yelling his name.
Max slunk toward the farmer and started to moan.
"Bad dog!" the man said in a stern, angry tone.

"You're too old," he sighed, rubbing Max's ears.
"Time to a train a new pup," said the farmer in tears.
Max whimpered sadly; his master was right.
Who would feel safe with him on guard at night?

For many dark hours, Max lay awake sleepless,
Thinking, "What will become of me now that I'm useless?"
Then he heard a small voice (did it come from a flea?)
Say, "You are only useless if you let yourself be."

It was later that week when more trouble went down.
The farmer had gone on some business to town.
When Max saw the farmer's house catch afire,
He knew that the pups' situation was dire.

He leapt into the house and through the great blaze,
He found all the pups in a black, smoky haze.
He saved every pup, from the thin to the stout,
And kept them all safe till the flames were put out.

The farmer came back and brought firemen round.
They kept the house from being burnt to the ground.
When the farmer found Max with the pups safe and sound,
He rubbed his ears and said, "You gutsy old hound,"

"I see you've still got your touch after all."
And Max lifted his chin and stood extra tall.
No one wins every time; it just cannot be done,
But the one who keeps trying wins in the long run. ○

6. What is the poem "Max's Story" MOSTLY about?

   Ⓐ a dog who becomes friends with a fox

   Ⓑ a dog who must accept that a new puppy is taking his place

   Ⓒ a dog who proves that he can still do his job well

   Ⓓ a dog's friendship with the chickens that he guards

7. Read these lines from the poem:

When Max saw the farmer's house catch afire /
He knew that the pups' situation was dire.

   What does the word *dire* probably mean?

   Ⓐ uncomfortable

   Ⓑ terrible

   Ⓒ getting better

   Ⓓ not clean

8. Max thinks that he is useless because

   Ⓐ his owner says that he is.

   Ⓑ he can't keep up with the pups.

   Ⓒ he can't keep up with the fox.

   Ⓓ he lets a fox into the chicken coop.

9. How does Max prove that he is still a good guard dog?

   Ⓐ He chases the chickens out of the coop.

   Ⓑ He runs to find the firemen when the fire starts.

   Ⓒ He chases after the fox and saves the chicken it took.

   Ⓓ He rescues all the pups from the burning house.

10. What is the main idea of this poem?

   Ⓐ Never let a fox guard the chicken coop.

   Ⓑ You can't teach an old dog new tricks.

   Ⓒ The one who keeps trying wins in the end.

   Ⓓ It is best to quit while you are ahead.

Directions *Read this article about tornadoes. Then answer questions 11 through 17.*

Tornadoes: The Most Violent Storms
by Femi Wilson

There are as many as one thousand tornadoes each year in the United States. Most of these are short-lived, relatively weak storms. They do damage, but in a fairly small area. Some tornadoes, however, are very powerful. These tornadoes can be terribly dangerous. They can destroy homes, cars, power lines, trees, and buildings, sometimes for miles around.

Tornado Facts

Tornadoes are violent windstorms. Tornadoes occur when there is a very strong spinning updraft, or rising column of air, inside a severe thunderstorm called a **super cell.** When the column of spinning air drops down out of thunderstorm clouds and touches the ground, a tornado forms. The stronger the tornado, the faster the winds blow. The wind speed of a tornado can range from forty to more than three hundred miles per hour.

Tornadoes are most likely to form in the following conditions:

- when warm and humid air at low levels mixes with cold air above it,
- when dry air is present in middle levels of the atmosphere, and
- when winds are changing speed and direction at different altitudes, or levels of the atmosphere.

The United States has more tornadoes than any other country. Within the United States, the Midwest has the most tornadoes. This region is often called "Tornado Alley." Tornadoes also happen frequently in the South and somewhat less frequently in the North. Tornadoes can happen at any time of the year. In the South and Midwest, however, they happen most often in the spring. Farther north, they occur mainly in the summer. Most tornadoes form in the afternoon and evening hours.

There are several signs that a tornado is likely. Large hail might fall, and the sky often turns dark or greenish. Some tornadoes are easy to see. Others are blocked by storm clouds. If visible, a tornado looks like a dark moving funnel. The funnel must be touching the ground to be considered officially a tornado. Scientists are still not exactly sure how to tell where tornadoes will form. Many people are working very hard to learn how to forecast tornadoes.

Tornadoes do damage in two main ways. First, powerful winds can damage anything in their path. Second, tornadoes pick up many objects as they move along the ground. Whether these objects are small or very large, they can cause a lot of damage when flying

NOAA Photo Library, NOAA Central Library; OAR/ERL/National Severe Weather Storms Laboratory (NSSL)

through the air at high speeds. The debris may be blown around at speeds up to one hundred miles per hour.

Tornado Safety Tips

Tornadoes occur in many parts of the United States. You may live in an area where tornadoes are likely to take place. If so, there are some important things you should know.

Tornadoes can form quickly and move very fast. Be prepared and plan ahead! Talk with your family to develop a plan in case there is a tornado. Figure out where you will go and how you will get in touch with each other if you are separated. Choose a family friend or relative to call who lives outside your area. Memorize that person's number. This is the number you will call to let everyone know that you are all right.

Be sure to have emergency supplies in your home. You may have to live without electric power and telephones. You may not be able to get fresh water or food. Use this checklist to make an emergency kit:

- portable, battery-operated radio
- flashlights
- extra batteries for radio and flashlights
- first aid kit/medicines
- food and water
- a can opener (non-electric)
- money/credit cards

Make sure to keep your ears open for tornado warnings on the radio and TV. If you are in a building when a tornado strikes, go quickly into the basement. If there is no basement, go into a closet or a hallway without windows. If that

GO ON

is not possible, get into the center of a room. Stay away from windows. Get under a heavy piece of furniture. Protect your head and neck with your arms.

If you are in a mobile home, leave as quickly as possible. Mobile homes can tip over and be crushed or ripped apart easily in a tornado. Try to find some shelter that has a solid foundation. Avoid large open buildings.

If you are not near a building, then find the best low shelter that you can. If you are in a car, get out. Go under an overpass, if there is one nearby, or lie down in a ditch or low-lying area if there is no shelter around. Stay as far away from power lines as possible. Remember that a strong tornado can roll over or even pick up a car.

The most important thing that you can do to protect yourself from

NOAA Photo Library, NOAA Central Library; OAR/ERL/National Severe Weather Storms Laboratory (NSSL)

tornadoes is to be informed. Have a plan of action in case of a tornado. It may not be possible to avoid tornadoes completely. However, if you know what to do when you see one coming, you are much more likely to stay safe. ○

11. What is the purpose of the article?

    Ⓐ to explain what tornadoes are, where they occur, and how to protect yourself from them

    Ⓑ to explain how scientists forecast when tornadoes are going to occur

    Ⓒ to tell the story of what happened when a tornado struck a small town

    Ⓓ to describe the areas of the country in which tornadoes are most likely to occur

12. In order for a funnel of wind to be considered officially a tornado, which of the following must happen?

    Ⓐ The funnel's wind speed must reach more than two hundred miles per hour.

    Ⓑ The funnel must be very dark and easy to see.

    Ⓒ The funnel must occur in the afternoon or evening.

    Ⓓ The funnel must be touching the ground.

13. Which of these statements from the article is an opinion?

    Ⓐ "Tornadoes are violent wind storms."

    Ⓑ "Tornadoes can form quickly and move very fast."

    Ⓒ "The most important thing that you can do to protect yourself from tornadoes is to be prepared."

    Ⓓ "Within the United States, the Midwest has the most tornadoes."

14. What should you do if you are in a car when a tornado occurs?

    Ⓐ Pull over and stay in the car until help comes.

    Ⓑ Pull over, get out, and find the closest shelter.

    Ⓒ Keep going, but drive away from the tornado.

    Ⓓ Keep going, but drive toward the tornado.

15. What is "Tornado Alley"?

    Ⓐ a place where tornadoes are studied

    Ⓑ the place where you should go if a tornado occurs

    Ⓒ the name of a folk song about a tornado

    Ⓓ the area of the country where tornadoes most often occur

16. In the Midwest, at what time of year do tornadoes most often occur?

Ⓐ fall

Ⓑ winter

Ⓒ spring

Ⓓ summer

17. The article tells some things you and your family can do to protect yourselves if you live in an area where a tornado might occur.

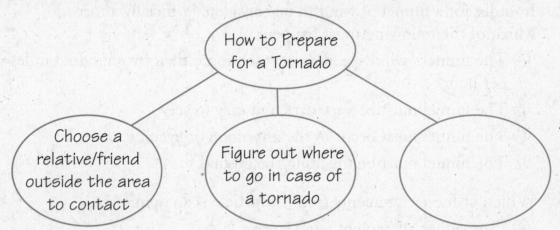

Which information from the article belongs in the empty circle in the word web above?

Ⓐ Stay as far away from power lines as possible.

Ⓑ Get under a heavy piece of furniture.

Ⓒ Make a kit with emergency supplies.

Ⓓ Leave the mobile home immediately.

Directions *Read this article about a girl who lives in the rain forest in Brazil. Then answer questions 18 through 23.*

In the Rain Forest
by Nhakaykep

My family lives in a thatched-roof hut in the rain forest of Brazil. We are part of a native tribe called the Kayapo. Our village is on the banks of the Xingu River, which runs into the Amazon, the biggest river in the world. Here it is warm year round.

Most of the food we eat comes from the river and forest. My father and brother catch fish in the river. (The men used to use bows and arrows to catch fish, but now they use hooks and lines.) Sometimes they kill alligators for us to eat. My sisters and I collect fruits and herbs from the forest and water from the village well. We also grow some food. To earn money for the tribe, my father helps to press oil from Brazil nuts. We sell the Brazilnut oil to foreign companies.

In school we learn Portuguese, which is the language of Brazil. We also learn Kayapo, the language of our people. At home, however, we are only allowed to speak Kayapo. My mother says it is very important to remember and practice the language and customs of our ancestors. One custom that I am learning from my mother and the other women is how to make medicines from the plants in the forest.

Another custom that my people follow is to paint our faces and bodies. We make the paint from plants that grow in the forest. We use mostly red and black paint, and sometimes a little white. Our body paint is not just for decoration. It shows important information about us.

The type of design we wear shows which age group we are in or which ritual we are about to perform. For example, my brother wears the simple red and black stripes that the young boys wear.

Girls who are old enough to marry wear wide black stripes on their thighs, upper body, and arms. It will be a few more years before I become a "black-thighed one," as we call the older girls. My mother has already begun to teach me how to paint the fancy designs that married women wear. When I am older, I will get to paint designs on my brother before important ceremonies. This is the special job of sisters.

At one time, young Kayapo men wore lip plugs, but this custom is not practiced as much anymore. In the past, when a boy reached puberty, he traded in the beads that young boys wear for a lip plug. A cut would be made in his lower lip and a small wooden disc would be placed in the hole. (At this time, boys also start to grow their hair long, a symbol of strength.) As the boys grew, they would gradually receive larger lip plugs. Finally, when the young males had proven themselves to be men, they would be given an adult-sized lip plug. Many of the younger men do not wear lip plugs anymore, however, because they are uncomfortable. They also make it difficult to speak Portuguese.

The nearest city is five hours away by road. Much of the rain forest between my village and the city has been chopped down. Our area of the forest belongs to the tribe. It is illegal for loggers to chop down trees on our land, but many ignore the law. When I think about how the forest is disappearing, it makes me very sad. I do not want to move to the city, but we may

have to move there if the forest is destroyed and the river becomes more polluted. I would like to live here by the river for the rest of my life, the way my ancestors always have. ○

18. Why did the author write this article?

Ⓐ to describe the lifestyle and customs of the Kayapo

Ⓑ to explain which plants can be used to make medicines

Ⓒ to explain how to fish in the Amazon River

Ⓓ to describe how to put on body paint for a ceremony

19. What custom is Nhakaykep learning from her mother and the other women of her tribe?

Ⓐ how to catch fish in the Xingu River

Ⓑ how to make lip plugs

Ⓒ how to cook alligator meat

Ⓓ how to make medicines from plants

20. What is one purpose of the Kayapo's body paint?

Ⓐ to show where they live

Ⓑ to show how old they are

Ⓒ to show how wealthy they are

Ⓓ to show what family they are part of

21. Nhakaykep is sad because

Ⓐ the government is trying to force the Kayapo to leave the forest.

Ⓑ her parents want to move to the city.

Ⓒ the forest is being chopped down.

Ⓓ another tribe is trying to force the Kayapo out of the forest.

22. According to Kayapo custom, what is the special job of sisters?

Ⓐ to paint the bodies of the babies in the village

Ⓑ to heal sick family members using medicinal plants

Ⓒ to paint their brothers' bodies before ceremonies

Ⓓ to teach their younger brothers the native dances

23. Which of the following is a central idea in the Kayapo culture?

Ⓐ It is important to preserve traditional customs.

Ⓑ Women should be able to do the same jobs as men.

Ⓒ People should not eat the meat of animals.

Ⓓ It is important to be able to speak many languages.

GO ON

Directions *Read this article about making maple syrup. Then answer questions 24 through 28.*

Maple Sugaring: A Springtime Tradition
by Tory Lucre

Can you imagine life without sugar? Americans today eat a lot of sugar—ten to fifteen times more than people did a few hundred years ago. Back then, sugar was very expensive and difficult to come by. Honey was the most common sweetener. But when they could get it, people satisfied their sweet tooth with maple syrup or maple sugar.

Native Americans taught the first European settlers how to tap sugar maple trees and turn the sap into syrup. Sugar maples are the best source of maple syrup. These trees are especially common throughout the eastern United States and Canada. Each year, people in these areas look forward to early spring, when they can head to the woods to go "maple sugaring."

Maple syrup can be harvested for only two to six weeks, from late February through March. This is the time of year when the temperature is usually above freezing during the day but falls below freezing at night. The warmer days cause the sap in the trees to flow freely. When the nights grow warm as well, and leaves begin to form on the trees, the sap stops flowing.

Above: Buckets for collecting sap. Right: A spigot inserted into the trunk of a maple tree.

Making maple syrup is a fairly simple, yet time-consuming process. First, the trees are tapped—a small hole is made in each tree, large enough for a tube or spigot to be inserted. (Don't worry; this process does not harm the tree.) The sap runs out of the spigots into buckets that have been placed to catch the sap. Then the sap must be boiled down to make maple syrup. If the sap is boiled long enough, it crystallizes and becomes maple sugar. One sugar maple tree produces about a gallon of sap. It takes forty to fifty gallons of sap—that's a lot of sap— to make just one gallon of syrup!

Nowadays, maple syrup is mass-produced with lots of expensive equipment. However, in areas where maple sugaring is a tradition, many people still make syrup the old-fashioned way. ○

Steps for making maple syrup:

1. Find a stand of sugar maple trees (a group of trees close together).

2. Tap each tree: make a hole about three inches deep, three feet above the tree's roots.

3. Insert a hollow tube, or spigot into the hole.

4. Hang a container, such as a bucket, from each tube or spigot to catch the sap as it oozes from the tree.

5. When the containers are full, empty them into a large, heavy pot. (Depending on how much syrup you want to make, you may need to repeat this step many times.)

6. Once you have gathered enough sap, bring it to a boil. Stir often to keep the sap from burning. (If it burns, the batch will be ruined.) Boil until the sap is as thick as syrup should be.

24. What is the main purpose of the article?

Ⓐ to tell about how the Native Americans made syrup

Ⓑ to describe the sweet foods that early settlers ate

Ⓒ to explain the history and process of making maple syrup

Ⓓ to persuade readers that they should eat less sugar

25. Here is a chart that shows how to make maple syrup. One of the steps is missing. From the answers below, choose the step that belongs in the blank space.

Ⓐ Stir constantly until thickened.

Ⓑ Hang buckets from the tubes.

Ⓒ Make holes three inches deep.

Ⓓ Wait for leaves to form on trees.

How to Make Maple Syrup
1. Find a stand of sugar maple trees.
2. Make holes in the trees.
3. Insert hollow tubes in the holes.
4.
5. Empty sap into large heavy pot.
6. Boil sap until thick enough.

26. To make maple sugar instead of maple syrup, you must

Ⓐ place the tap higher in the tree.

Ⓑ tap the trees in early September.

Ⓒ add other ingredients to the sap.

Ⓓ boil the sap for a longer time.

27. The way that it is used in the article, the word *stand* means

Ⓐ to be upright, rather than seated or lying down.

Ⓑ a piece of furniture for storing items, such as umbrellas.

Ⓒ a group of trees that are close together.

Ⓓ one's opinion or position on a topic.

28. Why must the sap be stirred constantly as it is boiling?

Ⓐ to prevent it from becoming too thick

Ⓑ to prevent it from burning

Ⓒ to prevent it from sticking to the pot

Ⓓ to prevent it from crystallizing

 Stop! End of Session 1

The rest of the test asks you to write about what you have listened to or read. Your writing will NOT be scored on your personal opinions. It WILL be scored on:

- how clearly you organize and express your ideas
- how accurately and completely you answer the questions
- how well you support your ideas with examples
- how interesting and enjoyable your writing is
- how correctly you use grammar, spelling, punctuation, and paragraphs

 Whenever you see this symbol, be sure to plan and check your writing.

GO ON

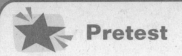

Session 2: Listening and Writing

Directions In this part of the test, you are going to listen to a story called "The Acorn and the Oak," by Mark Cheever. Then you will answer some questions about the story.

You will listen to the story twice. The first time you hear the story, listen carefully but do not take notes. As you listen to the story the second time, you may want to take notes. Use the space below and on the next page for your notes. You may use these notes to answer the questions that follow. Your notes on these pages will NOT count toward your final score.

Notes

Note to Teachers: This listening selection appears on pages 2–3 in the Teacher's Guide for AIM Higher! New York ELA Review.

Notes

Do NOT turn this page until you are told to do so.

29. Robin's father is very helpful to Robin in the story. In the box below, write three ways that Mr. Shulka helps Robin.

Mr. Shulka helps Robin by...
1. _____ _____
2. _____ _____
3. _____ _____

30. How does Robin's brother, Nick, treat her at the end of the story compared with the way that he treats her at the beginning of the story? Why does he treat her differently?

_____

_____

_____

_____

_____

_____

_____

Planning Page

You may PLAN your writing for question 31 here if you wish, but do NOT write your final answer on this page. Your writing on this Planning Page will NOT count toward your final score. Write your final answer beginning on the next page.

ANSWER

GO ON

31. Why does Robin's father tell her the story of the acorn and the oak? When Mr. Shulka says that Robin will grow like the oak, do you think he just means that she will get bigger? In what ways does Robin grow in the story? How can you tell that she has grown?

In your answer, be sure to

- explain why Robin's father tells her the story of the acorn and the oak

- describe the ways in which Robin grows in the story

- use details from the story to explain how you can tell that Robin has grown

 Check your writing for correct spelling, grammar, and punctuation.

_____

_____

_____

_____

_____

_____

_____

_____

Stop! End of Session 2

Session 3: Reading and Writing

Directions In this part of the test, you are going to read a story called "Little Bird That Hums" and an article called "Amazing Hummingbirds." You will answer questions 32 through 35 and write about what you have read. You may look back at the story and the article as often as you like.

Little Bird That Hums
based on Native American legend

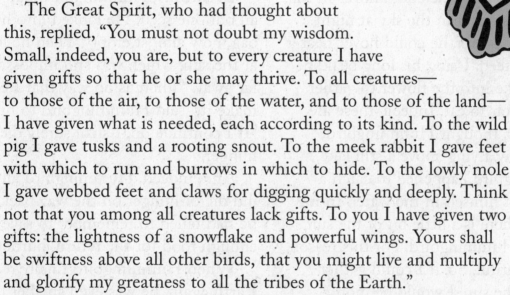

As you may know, the Great Spirit, after He made all the birds, had a few tiny scraps of feathers left over. Not wanting to waste anything, He made these into a very, very tiny bird, hardly big enough for a child's toy.

The tiny bird said, "Thank you for giving me life, but I am so small that I shall not last long. Hawk or Eagle will surely pluck me up and swallow me in a single gulp."

The Great Spirit, who had thought about this, replied, "You must not doubt my wisdom. Small, indeed, you are, but to every creature I have given gifts so that he or she may thrive. To all creatures— to those of the air, to those of the water, and to those of the land— I have given what is needed, each according to its kind. To the wild pig I gave tusks and a rooting snout. To the meek rabbit I gave feet with which to run and burrows in which to hide. To the lowly mole I gave webbed feet and claws for digging quickly and deeply. Think not that you among all creatures lack gifts. To you I have given two gifts: the lightness of a snowflake and powerful wings. Yours shall be swiftness above all other birds, that you might live and multiply and glorify my greatness to all the tribes of the Earth."

Hummingbird tried out his wings. Indeed, he could beat them so fast that they became a blur and made a steady hum, which is why he is called the bird that hums, or Hummingbird.

"Great are these gifts," said Hummingbird. "But how shall I attract a mate, for I am so drab and unappealing?"

"That, too, I have thought of," said the Great Spirit. "Fly to that clearing." The little bird flew to the clearing, where the sun shone through the forest canopy. The moment the sun hit his wings, Hummingbird shone brilliantly, in purple and green.

"I have placed a little bit of the sun in your feathers, so that when you fly into sunlight, you will shine in glory," said the Great Spirit.

"Indeed, I am beautiful," cried Hummingbird with joy.

"All things have their beauties," said the Great Spirit, "if you look at them in the right way."

And so Hummingbird went out into the world. After a while, he became hungry. He found that he could beat his wings so fast that he could hover in the air, as stars hover in the sky at night. Using this power, he could hover near a flower to feed. Using his long beak, he would poke into the flower to gather sweet nectar to eat. Indeed, these are great gifts, thought Hummingbird.

One day, flying above a still lake, Hummingbird happened to catch a glimpse of himself in the water. In my feathers there is a little bit of the sun, thought Hummingbird. For this reason, I am beautiful. So, if I could gather more of the sun, I would be more beautiful still. Then and there, he decided to fly off to reach the sun.

He began to prepare for his journey. First, he found a large leaf, and he folded it into a bundle. Into the bundle he placed all the seeds he could find, until the bundle was so heavy that he could barely lift it. Off Hummingbird flew, heading toward the sun, carrying the bundle of seeds in his beak. Each day, he would take one seed from the bundle and continue flying. And each day, no matter how far Hummingbird flew, the sun still seemed the same size—a small, bright orb very, very, very far away.

Eventually, Hummingbird had eaten all but one seed. He looked into his leaf bag, now almost empty. Then he looked at the sun, which was still impossibly far away. "There is no way that I can make it," said Hummingbird to himself. "If I continue on, I shall surely die of hunger."

And, indeed, Hummingbird almost did die of hunger on the way back, for he had failed to remember to save enough food for the return journey.

When Hummingbird finally reached Earth again, he was even smaller than he started out to be, and he remains that tiny to this day. Because he is so hungry, he eats from morning to night, but he never gains an ounce. ○

32. Fill in the chart below by listing three gifts that the Great Spirit gave to the hummingbird. Then explain the purpose of each gift. (Hint: the first two gifts have the same purpose.)

Gifts to Hummingbird	Purpose of Gifts
1.	
2.	
3.	

33. Where does Hummingbird decide to go and why? Is his journey successful? Why or why not?

_____

_____

_____

_____

_____

_____

GO ON

Amazing Hummingbirds
by Pablo Estevez

Hummingbirds truly are amazing creatures. They are the smallest birds in the world. The smallest of all hummingbirds, the bee hummingbird of Cuba, weighs only 2.2 ounces. For comparison, a penny weighs 3.3 ounces. The bee hummingbird is about the same weight as two paper clips! And it is about the size of—you guessed it—a bee.

To watch them fly, you would think that hummingbirds are little acrobats. They can fly right, left, straight up, straight down, backward, and upside down. They can also hover in the air, flapping their wings very, very quickly in a figure-eight. In normal flight, a ruby-throated hummingbird flaps its wings about fifty-five times each second and travels at twenty-five miles per hour. When hovering, hummingbirds have been known to flap their wings two hundred times per second! This is too fast for the human eye to follow. When a hummingbird hovers, we see nothing more than a blur around its little body.

Photo: U.S. Fish & Wildlife Service/Dean E. Biggins

Hummingbirds use up a lot of energy flapping their wings so fast. That is why they must eat constantly—every ten minutes, all day long. In a day, a hummingbird will consume two-thirds of its body weight. A hummingbird trapped in a garage without food can starve to death in an hour! Hummingbirds eat flower nectar, tree sap, insects, and pollen. People often put out hummingbird feeders containing a syrup made of four parts water and one part sugar. Then they sit back to enjoy the show as hummingbirds hover outside the window to feed. ○

34. In the boxes below, write three facts about hummingbirds that you learned from the article.

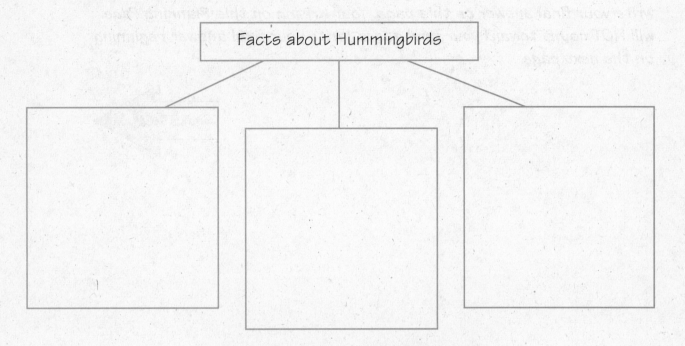

Facts about Hummingbirds

GO ON

Planning Page

You may PLAN your writing for question 35 here if you wish, but do NOT write your final answer on this page. Your writing on this Planning Page will NOT count toward your final score. Write your final answer beginning on the next page.

35. Myths and legends like the story "Little Bird That Hums" are often meant to describe or explain real things in nature. However, these stories also have parts that are not realistic. Based on what you know about hummingbirds from the article, which details about Hummingbird in the story are real, and which details are made up?

In your answer, be sure to

- explain which details about Hummingbird are real (which ones match the facts in the article)

- explain which details about Hummingbird are made up

- use examples from BOTH stories to support your answer

Check your writing for correct spelling, grammar, and punctuation.

_____

_____

_____

_____

_____

_____

_____

_____

_____

_____

_____

GO ON

_____

_____

_____

_____

_____

_____

_____

_____

_____

_____

_____

_____

_____

_____

_____

Stop! End of Test

Unit 1
Test-Taking Strategies

Read the following story about a boy who never studied. Then answer the questions that follow the story. At the end of the unit, you will be asked to come back to these questions to check your work and correct it, if necessary.

Campfire Stories

by Drew Johnson

Jacob's parents had gone inside their tent. Christa's parents were sitting on chairs near the lake. The four children sat around the still-burning campfire. Christa, her little sister Amelia, and Jacob's little brother Justin all had their faces turned toward Jacob. Jacob was just finishing his story.

"Finally, the fog lifted. The first light of dawn broke through the darkness. The two people looked around to see what had been scratching on their car door all night. Do you know what they found stuck in the passenger side door?" Jacob made his voice as low and spooky as possible.

"It was a metal hook—the same hook that the escaped madman wore in place of his missing hand." Jacob finished his story and waited for the screams.

The others stared at him silently.

"Scary story, huh?" he asked.

Amelia yawned. Justin scratched his ear. Christa looked as if she were falling asleep.

Amelia said, "Jacob, that story's not scary. It's just old. I've heard it a million times."

Justin agreed. "Yeah, we need some new stories. The old ones don't scare me at all."

Christa was eleven, a year older than Jacob. The younger children looked to her for help. Christa stared into the fire for a couple of minutes.

"OK," she said, "I've got a new story for you. And believe me, it's scary."

The kids scooted closer to Christa. "What's it called? What's it called?" asked Amelia.

Christa said, "Listen, and I'll tell you. This story is called 'The Test That Would Not End.'

"You see, there once was a kid named Milo Nails. Milo was the coolest kid in the entire fourth grade. Milo was so cool that he could wear bright orange socks and make them look good. No one I know could wear orange socks without looking like a complete dork—except for Milo.

"All the kids liked him. All the guys wanted to be like him. You would've thought Milo was perfect, but he wasn't. You see, Milo had a flaw. He never studied. Ever.

"Sure, Milo would listen in class. He would read the assigned textbooks, but he would never study or prepare for a test. While most kids were studying for a big test, Milo would go to the mall. You could see those orange socks walking around the Food Court each night before a test. Milo's grades weren't great, but he got by well enough to pass most tests . . . until that fateful day in Mr. Bingham's class.

"It was a simple reading exam," Christa explained. "Most students had no trouble with it. Milo flipped casually through the test, answering questions, but then he noticed that something odd was happening. Each time Milo completed a page of the test, two more pages appeared. Milo answered the questions as best he could, but they just kept coming. He wore out both of his No. 2 pencils. He started sweating really badly. All the other kids had long since finished, but Milo's test was bigger than ever.

"Then he sensed Mr. Bingham standing over him. His teacher seemed to have grown larger, and he was looking down on Milo with an evil grin.

"'You must not have studied last night, Milo,' Mr. Bingham's deep voice boomed. 'You see, this is a special test. For anyone who did not study, this test will never end!' Then Mr. Bingham threw back his head and let out an eerie, chilling laugh.

"For the first time ever, Milo lost his cool. All his classmates were shocked. The usual Milo was gone. They found themselves looking at a freaked-out, sweaty kid with goofy orange socks.

"No one knows what happened to Milo," Christa continued. "After that day, he was never seen again. Sometimes, though, you might catch a glimpse of orange socks in the school library. That's the ghost of Milo, studying."

Christa finished her story. The only sound was the crickets chirping. None of the children said a word. Silently, they all went into their tent together.

Ten minutes later, Jacob's parents noticed a lantern glowing inside the kids' tent. Looking in, Jacob's dad saw all four children staring at something on the ground. It appeared to be a book.

Jacob's mom looked at her watch. "It's 9:45 on a Saturday night. What are you kids doing?" she asked.

Jacob, Justin, and Amelia looked at her with serious faces. "We're studying," they said. ○

Your Turn

Exercise A *Answer the following questions. Write your answers in complete sentences.*

1. **A. Recalling Details**

What happens in the last part of Jacob's story?

_____

_____

_____

B. Interpreting Details

Why are none of the kids scared by Jacob's story?

_____

_____

_____

2. **A. Recalling Details**

Christa notes that Milo Nails wears unusual clothing. What does he wear that is unusual?

_____

_____

B. Interpreting Details

All characters have some strengths and some weaknesses. Name one strength and one weakness in Milo's character.

_____

_____

_____

_____

Exercise B *Do you think the kids are scared by Christa's story? Why or why not? (HINT: Think about what the kids do right after hearing the story. Does this show that the kids are scared, or does this show that they are not scared at all?)*

Write your answer in a paragraph on your own paper. Revise your paragraph using the Revision Checklist on page 196. Then copy the paragraph onto the lines below.

_____

_____

_____

_____

_____

_____

_____

_____

_____

_____

_____

Chapter 1
This Is Only a Test
Taking Tests

Poor Milo Nails. He should have known how important it is to study for tests. Tests are everywhere. You may think that you have to take a lot of tests now, but you will have to take even more tests in the future. You will have to take tests to move from one grade to the next. If you want to go to college, you will have to take other tests. Everyone who has a driver's license has to pass a test. If you want to become a hairdresser, a lawyer, a truck driver, or a doctor, you will have to pass a test. The sooner you learn how to prepare for tests, the better.

Learning about tests can help you to do better on them. This chapter will describe some basic items that commonly appear on tests. Understanding these items should help you to become a better test-taker.

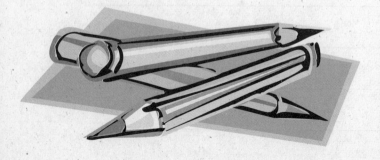

Understanding Test Questions

There are two main types of question that appear on many tests. These are

• multiple-choice questions and
• written-response questions.

Here is an example of a multiple-choice question:

1. Who is the oldest child in "Campfire Stories"?
   Ⓐ Amelia
   Ⓑ Christa
   Ⓒ Jacob
   Ⓓ Justin

Most **multiple-choice questions** have two parts—the leader line and the answer choices. The **leader line** asks a question. In this case, the leader line is "Who is the oldest child in 'Campfire Stories'?" The possible **answers** are listed under the leader line, next to letters. There are usually three or four choices. The example above has four choices. Generally, the directions will ask you to choose the best answer. Make sure you read the directions carefully to see how to mark your answer choice.

Many students get nervous during tests. They try to rush through the questions quickly. Rushing leads to careless errors, so slow down. Read the directions carefully. Make sure that you understand each question. Look at all the answer choices before you decide which answer is the best. First, cross out answers that are obviously wrong. Then pick the best answer from the ones that are left.

Look at the sample question on the previous page. Suppose you remember that the oldest child is a girl. This means that you can cross out choices C and D, because these are the boys. There are only two choices left, A and B. If you remember which girl is older, go ahead and answer the question. If not, go back and look at the story again. Scan the story quickly to find the names of the two girls. Whenever you see one of the girls' names, read the words around the name to see if the girl's age is mentioned. You should be able to find out which answer choice is correct. If you cannot find the answer, take a guess between choice A or B. You have a fifty-fifty chance of getting the right answer, which is B (Christa).

Here are some tips for answering multiple-choice questions:

How to Answer Multiple-Choice Questions

1. If you cannot find the answer to a question, go on to the next question. You can always come back later to the one you cannot answer. Do not forget to come back, though.

2. Pay attention to key words in directions, such as *most* or *except*.

3. If you are unsure of the correct answer, cross out answers that are obviously wrong first. Then choose the one that seems most likely to be correct from the ones that are left. (This was a technique used to answer the sample question above.)

4. Remember to choose the *best* answer to the question. If one answer is partly right but another is completely right, choose the one that is completely right.

Answering Written-Response Questions

Written-response questions require you to write out your own answer. These questions are usually more difficult than multiple-choice questions because there are no answers from which to choose. You must come up with the answer on your own.

There are two types of written-response question on the ELA exam:

- short-response
- extended-response

For more information on these types, see the next chapter.

When you get to a written-response question on a test, follow these steps:

1. Read the question slowly and carefully. Make sure that you understand it.

2. Ask yourself, "What kind of answer am I supposed to give?" The answer might be a word or two. It might be a few sentences. It might be several paragraphs.

3. Ask yourself where you need to get the information for your answer. Do you have to get it from something you have just read? (This is what you will have to do on the ELA test.) Do you have to get it from your own experience?

4. Gather your information. Make quick notes. Plan what you are going to say.

5. Write your answer clearly and simply, using complete sentences. If the question is about a reading passage, use details from the passage as evidence to support your answer.

6. Read over your answer. Make sure you have answered the question completely.

7. Check your answer for spelling, grammar, punctuation, and capitalization.

Here is a sample short-answer question that you might see on a test:

12. How do the other children react to Jacob's story? Are they frightened by it?

No answer is provided for this question, so it is harder than a multiple-choice question. You can still find the answer by going back and looking at the passage again. Remember that Jacob was telling his story at the beginning of the reading passage. Look back at that part of the passage. There you will find the description of the other kids' reactions to his story. Now you have the information you need to write your own answer to the question.

One Student's Response

The other children are not scared by Jacob's story. Justin scratches his ear. Christa looks as if she is falling asleep. Amelia yawns and tells Jacob that his story is "old" and that she has heard it "a million times."

First the student gives a one-sentence answer to the question. Then he (or she) backs up the answer with examples showing that the children are not scared.

Sometimes, written-response questions might ask for your opinion. An **opinion** is what you believe or feel about something. Here is an example:

13. Did you think that Christa's story was scary? Why or why not?

When you answer a question like this, give details and examples to support your opinion.

Sometimes, written-response questions require a long response. You might have to write several paragraphs. Here is a question like that:

14. Movies and books are very different. Explain, in your own words, the ways in which movies and books are similar and different.

Notice that this question requires you to use your own knowledge and experience in your answer.

Your Turn

Exercise A *Read each short passage on these two pages. Then fill in the circle next to the correct answer to each question.*

The okapi is a mysterious animal. Western scientists did not learn about the okapi until 1901. At first, some scientists thought the animal was related to the horse. The okapi is about the size and shape of a pony. The upper legs and hindquarters have horizontal stripes on them. This makes the okapi look like a dark zebra without most of its markings. Further study showed that the okapi is actually related to the giraffe. The okapi is much shorter than a giraffe, however, and its neck is not as long. It is difficult to learn more about the okapi. In the wild, the animal can be found only in one part of Zaire. This area of central Africa is a tropical jungle that is very hard to reach.

1. Which animal is most closely related to the okapi?
   - Ⓐ horse
   - Ⓑ pony
   - Ⓒ zebra
   - Ⓓ giraffe

2. When did Western scientists first learn about the okapi?
   - Ⓐ about a hundred years ago
   - Ⓑ about a thousand years ago
   - Ⓒ about fifty years ago
   - Ⓓ about five hundred years ago

"There it is," said my brother Mark. "It's hiding behind that tiny palm tree in the back."

"That's not an okapi," I said. My brother and I were visiting the Wendelhurst Zoo. We knew the zoo had just purchased an okapi. Some of the animals stood out in the open, but others liked to hide.

"Look at the sand and the palm trees, Mark," I said. "This exhibit looks like a desert. Okapis live in rain forests. Why would the zoo put an okapi in a desert?"

Mark was not convinced. "I saw its back legs. They had horizontal stripes. That means it's an okapi." Mark argued. "Maybe they put the okapi here because its own place wasn't ready yet."

Luckily, I found a way to end this argument. "Let's go ask him," I suggested, pointing to a person loading hay onto a golf cart. Mark and I walked over together to ask the zookeeper.

3. Who thinks the animal hiding probably isn't an okapi?
   Ⓐ the zookeeper
   Ⓑ the narrator (person telling the story)
   Ⓒ Mark
   Ⓓ Wendelhurst

4. How do the brothers settle their disagreement about the animal?
   Ⓐ Mark admits that he is wrong.
   Ⓑ The narrator admits that he is wrong.
   Ⓒ They decide to ask a person who works at the zoo.
   Ⓓ The animal comes out of hiding.

More ▶

Exercise B *Reread the two short passages on pages 48–49. Then answer the short-response question below.*

What kind of animal do you think is hiding at the zoo? Why do you believe this? Give reasons to support your answer.

_____

_____

_____

_____

_____

_____

Getting Ready to Take a Test

Studying is an important part of doing well on a test. It is not the only part, however. There are many other things you can do to improve your test-taking. Study the tips in the following chart.

How to Approach Standardized Tests

1. **Have confidence.** Believe in yourself and in your abilities. You will be surprised at what a positive attitude can do for your test scores.

2. **Build your vocabulary.** Having a good vocabulary will help you on most tests. The next time that you come across a word you do not know, write it down. When you have a chance, look up the word. Write down its meaning. Then try to use that new word in your own writing and speech. This method can build your vocabulary very quickly.

3. **Eat well and get enough rest.** Make sure to get enough sleep the night before a test. Eat healthy meals the night before and the morning of a test. Do not skip breakfast. Resting and eating well will help you do your best.

4. **Watch your watch.** If a test is timed, make sure that you have a watch of your own or that you can see a clock in the room. Try to answer every question on the test. By checking a watch or clock, you can keep from spending too much time on a single question.

5. **Do not let a difficult question get you down.** There may be some questions on a test that you do not understand. Most tests have a few difficult questions on them. Do not panic. Remember that the key is to get a *good* score. You do not need a *perfect* score. Reread the tough question. Try to figure out what is being asked. If you do this several times and you still don't get it, take a guess and fill in an answer.

6. **Take a break.** If you feel your brain starting to ache, take a minute or two to relax. Stretch your arms and legs if possible. Close your eyes for a moment and imagine something calm and peaceful. Then get back to the test once you are rested.

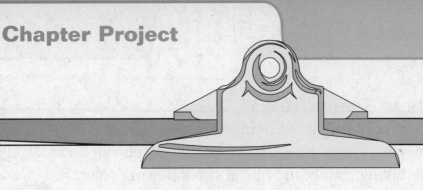

Chapter Project

You can understand tests better if you create one yourself. You may use additional paper if necessary.

✔ First, get together with two or three other students. Decide on a subject that interests you, such as ballet, baseball, a movie, a game, baking cookies, bowling, or a book you all enjoyed.

✔ Do some research on your subject. Then write at least two multiple-choice questions and one written-response question about it. Make sure there is only one correct answer for each multiple-choice question.

OUR TOPIC: _____

QUESTION #1: _____

Ⓐ _____ Ⓒ _____

Ⓑ _____ Ⓓ _____

QUESTION #2: _____

Ⓐ _____ Ⓒ _____

Ⓑ _____ Ⓓ _____

WRITTEN-RESPONSE QUESTION: _____

_____

_____

_____

Chapter 2

On Closer Examination

Understanding Your State Test

The state of New York wants all students to do well in school. To help make sure that students learn a lot in school, the state has created standards. **Standards** tell what you are supposed to learn in subjects like English and math. In New York, the standards for English are these:

Standard 1 Students will read, write, listen, and speak for information and understanding.

Standard 2 Students will read, write, listen, and speak for literary response and expression.

Standard 3 Students will read, write, listen, and speak for critical analysis and evaluation.

Standard 4 Students will read, write, listen, and speak for social interaction.

To find out whether kids are meeting the standards, the state created the ELA exams. **ELA** means "English Language Arts." The ELA exams test your ability to read, write, and listen. They test Standards 1 through 3. You will take an ELA exam each year in Grades 4 through 8.

What to Expect on the ELA Exam

When you take the ELA exam, you read and listen to short passages. Some will be literary passages. These are stories or poems. Others will be informative passages. These tell you facts or give you information about various subjects.

After reading one or two passages or listening to a passage, you will answer questions. There are several types of question on the exam.

For each **multiple-choice question,** you are given four possible answers. You must choose the answer that is correct.

For each **short-response question,** you must write a short response or fill in a chart. Your answer might be anything from one or two sentences to a full paragraph.

For each **extended-response question,** you must answer in a longer piece of writing. Usually, you will write more than one paragraph when you answer one of these questions.

How the ELA Exam Is Divided Up

The fourth-grade ELA exam is given in three parts. Here's what you will do in each part:

Session 1: Reading

—You will read four to six passages.

—You will answer twenty-eight multiple-choice questions about the passages.

—This part of the test covers Standards 1, 2, and 3.

Session 2: Listening and Writing

—You will listen to a short story.

—You will answer two short-response questions and one extended-response question about the story.

—This part of the test covers Standard 2.

Session 3: Reading and Writing

—You will read two passages. These will be related to each other in some way. They may be literary or informative.

—You will answer three short-response questions and one extended-response question about the passages.

—This part of the test covers Standard 3.

How the ELA Exam Is Scored

You will receive credit for each multiple-choice question that you answer correctly in the Reading section of the exam. Your short and extended responses will be scored in the following way:

• You will receive one score, ranging from 0 to 4, for the two short responses and one extended response that you write for the Listening and Writing section of the exam.

• You will receive another score, ranging from 0 to 4, for the three short responses and one extended response that you write for the Reading and Writing section of the exam.

• You will also receive one writing mechanics score, ranging from 0 to 3. This score will be based on the two extended responses that you write. Your short-response answers will not count toward this score.

To receive a top score of 4, your short and extended responses (taken as a whole from each test session) must do the following:

- Fulfill all the requirements of the task (In other words, each response must answer all of the questions or follow all of the directions given in the prompt.),
- Address the theme or key elements of the text,
- Show an insightful interpretation of the text,
- Make connections beyond the text (In other words, you must make connections to other things you've read or heard.),
- Develop ideas fully with thorough elaboration,
- Use relevant and accurate examples from the text.

In addition, your extended response must do the following:

- Establish and maintain a clear focus,
- Show a coherent and logical sequence of ideas through the use of transitions and other devices,
- Be fluent and easy to read, with vivid language and a strong voice,
- Have a sophisticated style, using varied sentence structure and challenging vocabulary.

To receive a top score of 3 in writing mechanics,

- Your extended responses must contain few, if any, errors. There should be no errors that make the writing difficult to understand.
- Your grammar, syntax (sentence structure), capitalization, and punctuation must be mostly correct.
- Any misspellings should be minor. If there are any misspellings, they should be difficult words that show you took a risk including sophisticated vocabulary.

In this book, you will learn and practice skills you need to read and write well. You will learn how to read actively. You will learn how to take notes on what you read and hear. You will learn how to answer multiple-choice questions, short-response questions, and extended-response questions. You will also learn how to write various kinds of essays. Of course, the best way to prepare for the exam is to practice reading, writing, listening, and taking notes all year long. Reading and writing regularly is key. If you practice these skills often on your own, you will succeed not just on the ELA exam but in life as well.

Return to the exercises at the beginning of the unit. Check your work and fix it if necessary. Give the exercises to your teacher for grading.

Unit 2
Reading Skills Review

Read the following passage about dogs. Then answer the questions that follow the passage. At the end of the unit, you will be asked to come back to these questions to check your work and correct it if necessary.

Dogs for Work, Play, and Show

by Sylvia Nagy

For thousands of years, dogs have been people's best friends in the animal world. Dogs make great pets. They also help people in many ways.

Whoever you are, there is probably a dog that is right for you. Around the world, there are over 400 different kinds, or **breeds,** of dog. The American Kennel Club (AKC) recognizes 148 breeds. The different breeds can be put into seven official groups: sporting dogs, hounds, working dogs, terriers, toy dogs, herding dogs, and nonsporting dogs. The AKC also has a separate group for dogs that are relatively rare but are becoming more popular in the United States.

Golden Retriever

Cocker Spaniel

Irish Setter

Labrador Retriever

Alaskan Malamute

Doberman Pinscher

Great Dane

St. Bernard

Mastiff

Siberian Husky

Sporting dogs are bred to work outdoors. These dogs are bred for hunting and retrieving. They like lots of exercise and fresh air. Sporting dogs usually make great pets. Examples of sporting dogs include the cocker spaniel, the golden retriever, the Irish setter, and the Labrador retriever.

Hounds are also hunting dogs. They are very good at running. Some hounds can smell faint scents (smells) from really far away. Some are good at **tracking,** or finding a person or animal by following traces of a scent. Others are good at tracking using their sharp eyes. Examples of hounds include the Afghan hound, the beagle, the bloodhounds, the dachshund, and the greyhound. Bloodhounds are very good at tracking. Greyhounds are very good at running races.

Working dogs are big and strong. Some of them are used to pull sleds, carry packs, and perform rescues. Others are used to guard property or livestock. Popular working dogs are the Alaskan malamute, the Doberman pinscher, the Great Dane, the mastiff, the St. Bernard, and the Siberian husky. Huskies are often used as sled dogs. Mastiffs and St. Bernards are sometimes used as rescue dogs.

Afghan Hound

Greyhound

Dachshund

Beagle

Bloodhound

Jack Russell
Terrier

Scottish
Terrier

West Highland
White Terrier

Pekingese

Chihuahua

Yorkshire
Terrier

Pomeranian

Pug

Shih Tzu

Terriers are small and full of energy. They love to run about and play. Some common terriers are the Scottish terrier, the Jack Russell terrier, and the West Highland white terrier.

Toy dogs are tiny. Some are smaller than a cat. Although toy dogs may look like toys, they still need to be trained and cared for. They are kept as pets. People who live in small apartments often like toy dogs. A toy dog doesn't take up much room: It fits right in your lap. Examples of toy dogs include the Chihuahua, the Pekingese, the Pomeranian, the pug, the Shih Tzu, and the Yorkshire terrier.

Herding dogs are a special type of working dog. Herding dogs are good at watching and controlling sheep or cattle. Some herding dogs are the border collie, the collie, the German shepherd, the Old English sheepdog, and the Welsh corgi.

German
Shepherd

Border Collie

Old English
Sheepdog

Collie

Welsh Corgi

Nonsporting dogs is a group made up of a variety of dogs. These dogs don't fit easily into the other groups. Examples include the bulldog, the chow chow, the Dalmatian, the Chinese Shar-pei, the Lhasa apso, and the poodle.

The eighth group, the **miscellaneous dogs,** includes breeds you probably have never heard of. Do you know anyone who has a Black Russian terrier or a Plott hound? If these breeds become popular enough, they will join the breeds in the other groups on the AKC list.

In the past, people used dogs mostly for work. Dogs guarded houses. They herded sheep. They pulled sleds. They caught mice and rats. They helped with hunting. These days, however, most people keep dogs as pets. In 2004, there were over sixty-five million pet dogs in the United States! That's almost one dog for every five people!

Chow Chow

Poodle

Bulldog

Chinese Shar-pei

Lhasa Apso

Dalmatian

Plott Hound

Black Russian Terrier

Facts about the Interesting World of Dogs

- The largest dog ever known was an Old English mastiff named Zorba. This dog was 8 feet 3 inches long from the tip of his nose to the tip of his tail. He weighed 343 pounds.

- The world's smallest dog is a Chihuahua and Shih Tzu mix. It is less than 4 inches tall and weighs only about a pound.

- Some of the most famous dogs in the world are Barney (a Scottish terrier) and Spot (an English springer spaniel). They belong to George W. Bush. Buddy, a chocolate Labrador retriever, belonged to former President Bill Clinton and used to live in the White House.

- Terriers are now prized as pets. They are active little dogs that like to run and play. In the past, they were used to catch mice and rats.

- Americans spend more than one billion dollars a year on pet food.

- More than half a million dogs live in New York City alone.

- The fastest of all dogs is the greyhound. It can run at up to forty-two miles per hour.

- Seeing Eye dogs can help blind people to cross streets safely. German shepherds, Labrador retrievers, and golden retrievers are often used as Seeing Eye dogs.

- Dogs are closely related to foxes, wolves, and coyotes. ○

Exercise A *Fill in the circle next to the correct answer to each question.*

1. How many breeds of dog does the American Kennel Club recognize?
   Ⓐ 400 breeds
   Ⓑ 300 breeds
   Ⓒ 248 breeds
   Ⓓ 148 breeds

2. Which breed is the fastest of all dogs?
   Ⓐ mastiff
   Ⓑ cocker spaniel
   Ⓒ greyhound
   Ⓓ Labrador retriever

3. Which of the following dogs would be the BEST choice if you lived in a small apartment in the city?
   Ⓐ St. Bernard
   Ⓑ Chihuahua
   Ⓒ Dalmatian
   Ⓓ golden retriever

4. Although terriers are now prized as lively little pets, what purpose have they served in the past?
   Ⓐ They were often used as Seeing Eye dogs.
   Ⓑ They were known as great guard dogs.
   Ⓒ They were used to pull sleds and rescue people.
   Ⓓ They were used to catch mice and rats.

5. Which type of dog would the police MOST LIKELY use to try to track down a missing person?
   Ⓐ greyhound
   Ⓑ Great Dane
   Ⓒ bloodhound
   Ⓓ poodle

More ▶

Your Turn

Exercise B *Some people keep dogs simply as pets. Others depend on their dogs to do important work for them. Explain some of the ways that dogs help people. Use facts from the reading passage (including the fact sheet) to support your ideas. Write a paragraph on a separate piece of paper. Check your writing for errors in spelling, capital letters, and punctuation. Fix any mistakes. Then copy the final draft of your paragraph onto the lines below.*

_____

_____

_____

_____

_____

_____

_____

_____

_____

_____

_____

_____

_____

Chapter 3

Talking Back to Books

Active Reading

Before Reading: Previewing a Passage

When you come across a reading passage on an exam, first **preview** it, or look ahead to see what it is about. When you **scan** a piece of writing, you look it over quickly to find specific parts. Begin your previewing by scanning to find these parts:

Scanning to Find Specific Parts

- The **title** is at the top of the first page. The title usually gives you a good idea of what the reading passage is about.
- The **author** is the person (or persons) who wrote the piece.
- **Headings,** or **subheads,** are little titles that sometimes label the parts of the text.
- The **introduction** is the first paragraph of the text. The introduction presents the main idea.
- **Illustrations** are pictures, drawings, or maps.
- **Captions** are words that explain an illustration or photograph. They are placed next to or under pictures.
- **Key words** are the important words in the text. Key words might stand out in **boldface,** in *italics,* or underlining.
- The **conclusion** is the last paragraph of the text. In the conclusion, the author sums up his or her ideas.

Look at the title, the name of the author, any headings in the text, the illustrations and captions, and any key words that are highlighted in special type. Take a quick look at the introduction and the conclusion. As you preview the passage, ask yourself what the story or article as a whole is about. What is the main idea? You may want to make up a list of questions called **prereading questions.** These are ones that you expect to be answered when you read the passage carefully.

Exercise A *Preview the following passage. Look at the title, the author's name, the headings, the illustrations and captions, and any key words. Look quickly at the introduction and the conclusion. Then, on a separate piece of paper, write three prereading questions about the passage. Your questions should be ones that you think the passage will answer when you read it carefully.*

The Father of All Traffic Laws
by H. S. Montgomery

Can you imagine what driving would be like if there were no traffic laws? When cars were invented, streets were a free-for-all. There were no speed limits. No one signaled for turns. Often people drove right down the middle of the road! In New York City, one person a day was killed in the busy streets. The streets were full of trolleys, bicycles, and wagons pulled by horses, as well as a number of cars. One day, a quiet man named **William Phelps Eno** introduced the traffic rules that made order out of the mess in the streets.

The Traffic Jam

William Phelps Eno grew up in a wealthy family in New York City. One day, when he was nine years old, William was stuck in traffic on Broadway near Grand Street for a half hour.

Traffic signs are one way to tell drivers where and when they should go.

"That very first traffic jam will always remain in my memory," he later recalled.

"There were only a dozen horses and carriages, but neither the drivers nor the police knew what to do. All that was needed was a little order to keep the traffic moving."

The Traffic Laws

After going to college, William Eno worked in New York City. When he was in his early forties, he became very rich. He decided to give his time to the traffic problem.

William wrote an article for a magazine called *Rider & Driver*. The article introduced the traffic rules that we know today: "Stay to the right. Signal for turns and when slowing down or stopping. Drivers should be licensed." Eno also suggested speed limits, traffic signs, taxi stands, special traffic police, and traffic tickets.

The Father of Traffic Regulation

The rules were put to use in New York City in 1903. They were a success. After people started using the rules, traffic flowed better, even on crowded streets. Eno reported that he saw no traffic "**blockade,**" or jam, that lasted more than a minute.

Eno worked hard to get other cities to use his traffic rules. Each year, he wrote two thousand letters and articles. He wrote six books on traffic control. He traveled the country and went to Europe nine times to speak about his ideas. England, France, and Italy all decided to use Eno's traffic **regulations,** or rules. However, it took twenty-five years before Washington, D.C., finally adopted them.

Before traffic rules, drivers just went anywhere in the road.

By the time William Eno died in 1945, he was called "The Father of Traffic Regulation." But Eno never got a driver's license. He never liked cars.

Exercise B *Now read the passage closely. See if you can answer the questions that you wrote for Exercise A.*

More ▶

Your Turn

Exercise C *Answer these questions in complete sentences. You may look back at the passage.*

1. What should you do before reading a story or article carefully?

   _____

2. What is the title of the story about traffic?

   _____

3. Who is the author of the story?

   _____

4. What is pictured in the two illustrations in the story?

   _____

   _____

5. Write two facts that you read in the captions.

   _____

   _____

6. Look back at the **boldfaced** words in the text. What do the words *blockade* and *regulations* mean?

   _____

   _____

7. How did William Eno convince people to use his traffic rules?

   _____

   _____

8. Which sentence in the introduction gives the main idea of the passage?

   _____

Active Reading

During Reading: Active Reading Strategies

Before reading a story, article, or chapter in a book, you should look it over to see what it is about. Then you should come up with questions about the reading. As you read, look for the answers to your questions and use the active reading strategies listed below:

Active Reading Strategies

Ask Questions	As you read, you should **ask questions** about what you are reading. Questioning will help you to figure out whether you agree with what the writer has to say. This will help you to notice if the writer has left out any important information. It will also help you to remember what you have read.
Visualize (Form Pictures in Your Mind)	As you read, you should try to **visualize,** or picture in your mind, what the writer is describing. You are much more likely to remember details, such as what a character looks like or where something happens, if you try to picture these things in your mind as you read.
Predict (Make Guesses about What Will Happen)	Try to **predict** about what will happen next in a story, or what an article will talk about. If you try to guess what will happen next, you are more likely to want to read on to find out whether you were right. The more you practice this skill, the better you will become at making the right predictions.

More ▶

Active Reading Strategies, contd.

Summarize

Have you ever finished reading a homework assignment only to find that you have no idea what you just read? It happens to everyone. A great way to make sure that you understand what you are reading is to stop and summarize. When you **summarize** a story, you tell what happened in your own words, using fewer words. As you read, stop every once in a while and ask yourself what has happened so far. If you cannot sum up what you have read, you should go back and reread it. If you find yourself having to go back and reread a lot, then you should stop more often to think about what you have read.

Make Connections

As you read, **think about what you already know** about the subject. Perhaps you have already learned about the subject at home or in school. Does what the writer is saying about the subject agree with what you already know? Also think about how the information is connected to your own life.

Exercise A *Read the passage below. As you read, make notes about the passage on the lines provided. Ask questions. Describe what you are picturing in your mind. Make guesses about what will happen. Summarize. Make connections. Some notes have already been added to help you get started.*

Baking a Good Enough Apple Pie

1 You don't have to be a really great chef (or a really great grandmother) to bake a good apple pie. Here's how you can make an apple pie that is good enough for most purposes. It might not win any 2 fairground pie-baking contests, but it will certainly win a few hearts.

The first and most important thing is choosing the right apples. That's an easy one: Nothing beats Granny Smiths. Sweet apples make terrible pies. Sweet apples fall apart and become mushy and lose all their flavor when baked. What you need for a good pie is apples that are downright sour, and Granny Smiths are about as sour as you can get from an ordinary supermarket or grocery. You will recognize Granny Smiths because of their green skin.

Next you need to buy some pie crusts. If you have ever had a piece of a truly great apple pie, then you know that the best pies have homemade crusts that are light and layered and flaky. But making good pie crusts is an art that not everyone has the time and interest to master. Buy some ready-made crusts. These days, most

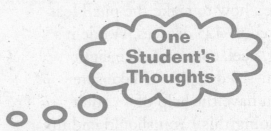

One Student's Thoughts

1. Predicting: This piece will give me step-by-step directions.

2. Connecting: I've been to fairs, but I've never seen a pie-baking contest.

Your Notes and Questions

_____

_____

_____

_____

_____

_____

_____

_____

_____

More ▶

_____

groceries and supermarkets carry them. The pie crust dough comes ready-made, wrapped in cellophane and boxed.

Here's how to make the pie: Heat your oven to 425 degrees. While it's heating, peel, core, and slice eight medium-sized apples. (Make sure that you have the help of an adult when doing this.) You should end up with about eight cups of apple slices. Try to keep the sizes of your slices even. I like thick slices, but slice them according to your taste, remembering that they will shrink as they bake.

In a large bowl, mix 2/3 cup of sugar, 1/4 cup of flour, 1/4 teaspoon of ground nutmeg, 3/4 teaspoon ground cinnamon, a pinch of salt, and (if you like) a pinch of allspice. Stir in your apples and mix until the slices are covered with spiced sugar. Sprinkle evenly with 1 tablespoon of lemon juice and mix again. If you like, add 1/4 cup of raisins or dried currants as well.

Unfold one of your ready-made pie crusts. Use a rolling pin to roll it out a bit so that it will droop slightly over the edges of your pie pan (which should be a glass pan about 9 inches in diameter and 3/4 of an inch deep). Lightly press the ready-made crust into your pie pan. Fill the crust with your apple mixture. Dot the filling with about little pieces (about 2 tablespoons in all) of margarine. Then place a second crust on top and crimp the edges all around to seal. Cut slits in the top or poke the top crust with a fork to allow steam to escape while the pie is breaking.

Bake 40 to 50 minutes or until the crust is golden brown. Let the pie cool before cutting and serving. Enjoy the praise of all the pie eaters among your friends and family! ○

More ▶

Your Turn

Exercise B *Try to answer the following questions without looking back at the passage. Write your answers in complete sentences.*

1. Why are sour apples better for making pies than sweet ones?

   _____

   _____

   _____

2. How is the crust of a truly great apple pie DIFFERENT from the crust of an OK apple pie?

   _____

   _____

   _____

3. What spices are used in apple pie?

   _____

   _____

   _____

4. How many crusts does this apple pie have?

   _____

   _____

   _____

5. What optional (not necessary) ingredients does this pie have?

   _____

   _____

   _____

Active Reading

During Reading: Dealing with Difficult Vocabulary

Once in a while, when reading, you will come across a word that you do not know. Usually, you can look up the difficult word in a dictionary, or you can ask someone what it means. When taking a test, however, you will have to figure out what the word means on your own. You can do this by using context clues and word parts.

Context Clues

You know what a **clue** is. It is a hint or a piece of evidence that helps you to figure something out. Often, you can figure out what a difficult word means by looking at its context. The **context** is the material around the word. Often, this material will give you clues to the meaning of the word. The following chart describes some types of context clue.

Common Context Clues

Restatements. A restatement gives the meaning of the word directly, using different words. A restatement is a definition. This is the easiest type of context clue.

> EXAMPLE: Mr. Santos is an expert in etymology—the history of words.

> EXAMPLE: Ms. Santos is a diplomat. She represents the United States government to a foreign country.

Etymology is the study of the history of words. A *diplomat* is someone who represents the government to a foreign country.

Examples. Examples are samples of the thing being described.

> EXAMPLE: This farmer raises various kinds of fowl, including chickens, turkeys, ducks, and geese.

Fowls are birds, such as chickens, turkeys, ducks, and geese, that are raised for food.

More ▶

Contrast. Sometimes the meaning of a word is made clear by contrasting it with something else. A contrast shows the differences between things.

EXAMPLE: Josie was extremely happy. Her brother, in contrast, was quite sullen.

The contrast tells you that *sullen* is the opposite of "extremely happy."

Comparison. Sometimes the meaning of a word is made clear by comparing it to something else. A comparison shows how things are alike.

EXAMPLE: Billy the Kid was a dastardly outlaw. Jesse James was likewise mean and cowardly.

The comparison tells you that *dastardly* means "mean and cowardly."

Inference. Sometimes you can figure out the meaning of a word by making an inference. An inference is a guess based upon general clues in the context.

EXAMPLE: Using a plane, Mr. Knatt removed shavings of wood from the back of the guitar neck.

Obviously, a *plane,* in this sense, is a tool for shaving wood.

For more information on using context clues, see Chapter 4, "I Think I've Got It! Reading Comprehension" pages 100–101.

Word Parts

Often you can figure out the meaning of a word by looking at its parts. Here are some common parts of words:

A **prefix** is a word part added to the beginning of a word. For example, you can add the prefix *micro–*, which means "small," to the word *manage*.

micro– + *manage* = *micromanage*

The new word means "to manage all the small things—the little details."

A **suffix** is a word part added to the end of a word. For example, you can add the suffix *–ling* to the word *duck*.

duck + *–ling* = *duckling*

The new word means "a small, or baby, duck."

A complete word to which another word part is added is called a **base word.** In the examples above, *manage* and *duck* are base words. Sometimes two base words are put together to make a **compound word.**

grape + *fruit* = *grapefruit*
key + *board* = *keyboard*

Some words use word parts that cannot stand alone as words but that carry the main meaning. These word parts are called **roots.** For example, the root *aqua* means "water." It appears in lots of words:

aqualung
aquamarine
aquarium
aquatic
aqueduct
aqueous
aquiculture

Suppose that you know that the root *aqua* means "water." You can then figure out that an *aqualung* is something that lets you breathe under water. You can figure out that if something is *aqueous*, it is "watery." A group of words that have the same root is called a **word family.**

Active Reading

The following charts give some examples of common prefixes, suffixes, roots, and word families.

Common Prefixes

Prefix	Meaning	Example
anti–	against	anti-American (against America)
auto–	self	automatic (happening by itself)
bi–	two	bicycle (two-wheeled vehicle)
co–, com–, con–	with	co-worker (person with whom one works)
de–	undo	defrost (take away frost)
ex–	from, out, past	ex-president (past president)
fore–	before, in front of	foretell (predict, or tell beforehand)
hemi–	half	hemisphere (half of a sphere or globe)
hyper–	over, beyond	hyperactive (overly active)
im–, in–	not, opposite of	infrequent (not frequent), impossible (not possible)
mal–	bad	malnutrition (bad or insufficient nutrition)
micro–	small	microscope (device for looking at small objects)
mono–	one	monorail (train that travels on one track, or rail)
non–	not, opposite of	nonfat (food or drink that does not contain fat)
over–	too much, extra	overload (put on too much weight; too much load)
post–	after	posttest (test taken after instruction)
pre–	before, in front of	prewar (before the war)
re–	again, back	replay (play again)
semi–	part, half	semicircle (half of a circle)
sub–	under, below	submarine (below the sea)
trans–	across, over, change	transcontinental (across the continent), transform (change from one form to another)
tri–	three	triweekly (three times a week)
un–	not, opposite of	unhinge (change or remove a piece of something so that it is not hinged)
uni–	single, one	unidirectional (moving in one direction only)

Common Suffixes

Suffix	Meaning	Example
-able, -ible	capable of, able to	*drinkable* (capable of being drunk)
-al	of, like	*magical* (like magic)
-ess	female	*lioness* (female lion)
-fold	multiplied by	*tenfold* (multiplied by ten)
-ful, full	full of	*harmful* (full of harm or danger)
-ic	like, similar to, having to do with	*angelic* (like an angel)
-ily	like, in the manner of	*happily* (in the manner of someone who is happy)
-ish	in the manner of	*childish* (in the manner of a child)
-ism	act, practice, doctrine, or theory of	*terrorism* (act of spreading terror), *communism* (Communist doctrine)
-less	without	*fearless* (without fear)
-ly	in the manner of	*calmly* (in a calm manner)
-ous	possessing, full of	*joyous* (full of joy)
-ward	in direction of	*westward* (in the direction of the west)
-y	full of, containing	*faulty* (containing one or more faults)

Suffixes That Form Nouns

Suffix	Meaning	Example
-er, -or	one who	*worker* (one who works)
-ing	thing resulting from an action	*painting* (what results when one paints)
-ion, -sion, -tion	act of, state of, thing resulting from	*perfection* (state of being perfect)
-ment	act of, state of, thing resulting from	*merriment* (state of being merry)
-ness	act of, state of, thing resulting from	*happiness* (state of being happy)

More ▶

Suffixes That Form Plurals of Nouns

Suffix	Meaning	Example
–s, –es	plural	*games, dishes* (more than one game, dish)

Suffixes That Make Verbs (Action Words) Past Tense

Suffix	Meaning	Example
–ed	past tense	*laughed* (laughing that took place in the past)

Suffixes Used for Comparisons

Suffix	Meaning	Example
–er	to compare two items	*longer* (as in "A nautical mile is longer than a mile.)
–est	to compare more than two items	*fastest* (as in "Light is the fastest thing in the universe.")

Some Common Roots and Word Families

Root	Meaning	Examples
anni, annu, enni	year	*anniversary, annual, bicentennial*
anim	living	*animation*
aud	hear, listen	*audible, auditorium*
auto	self	*autobiography*
bibl, biblio	book	*bibliography, Bible*
capt	take	*captive, capture*
chron, chrono	time	*chronological*
cred, creed	know, believe	*incredible*
dem, demo	people	*democracy, endemic*
duc, duct	carry, lead	*conduct, deduction*
fid, fide	faith, trust	*confidence, Fido* (dog's name)
fract, frag	break, part	*fracture, fragment*

More ▶

Root	Meaning	Examples
geo	Earth	*geology*
hydro, hydr	water	*hydrant, hydraulic, hydropower*
junct	join	*junction, conjunction*
log, logy	word, thought, study	*sociology, dialogue*
mort	death	*immortal, mortified*
patr, patri	father, country	*patron, patriarch, patriotic*
path	sadness, suffering	*pathological, sympathetic*
phil	love	*philanthropy, philharmonic*
phon, phone, phono	sound	*phonic, microphone, phonograph*
pod, pode	foot, footlike	*tripod*
psych, psycho	of the mind	*psychology*
sci	know	*conscious, science*
sen	old	*senior*
spec	see	*inspection, spectacle, speculate*
tele	far, across distance	*telegraph, telephone, teleportation*
therm, thermo	heat	*thermal, thermometer*
viv	alive, life	*revive, vivacious*
voc	call	*vocal*
vore	swallow, eat	*carnivore, voracious*

Exercise A *On the lines, write the meanings of the italicized words.*
Use context clues to figure out the meanings.

1. Ebony is a *rigid* wood. Balsa, in contrast, can easily be bent.

_____

2. The male lead in the play spoke so softly that the audience could barely hear him. The leading lady was also almost *inaudible*.

_____

3. Some well-known *scarabs* include the June bug and the dung beetle.

_____

4. I don't like *cloying* desserts. For example, the chocolate mousse was too rich and sweet.

_____

5. Prince Hamlet was wearing a *doublet*, a close-fitting, sleeveless jacket.

_____

Exercise B *After each word, tell what the prefix is, what the prefix means, and what the word as a whole means. Use the chart on page 78.*

1. bicycle

PREFIX: _____

MEANING OF PREFIX: _____

MEANING OF WORD: _____

2. unicycle

PREFIX: _____

MEANING OF PREFIX: _____

MEANING OF WORD: _____

3. tricycle

PREFIX: _____

MEANING OF PREFIX: _____

MEANING OF WORD: _____

Exercise C *Answer each question. Use the charts on pages 78–81.*

1. What is the meaning of the prefix *mal*–?

_____

2. What is the meaning of the suffix *–ous*?

_____

3. What is the meaning of the word *malodorous*?

_____

More ▶

Exercise D *Use the base words given below to write as many compound words as you can.*

ball	home	some
day	rise	sun
fall	shield	wind
foot	sick	work

1. _____
2. _____
3. _____
4. _____
5. _____

6. _____
7. _____
8. _____
9. _____
10. _____

Exercise E *Answer the questions on the lines provided.*

1. What prefix does the word *conscious* contain? What does that prefix mean?

   _____

2. What root does the word *conscious* contain? What does that root mean?

   _____

3. What do the prefix, root, and suffix in the word *conscious* mean when you put them together?

   _____

4. What does the prefix *im–* mean?

   _____

5. The word *mortal* means "one who will eventually die." What does the word *immortal* mean?

   _____

After Reading: Reflecting and Responding

After you read a passage, you need to reflect on it and respond to it. When you **reflect,** you think about your reading. When you **respond,** you react to the reading with your own ideas. Here are some specific ideas for what to do after reading:

Activities to Do After Reading

Reflect on the Reading

- Answer your prereading questions.
- Think about the main idea and supporting details in the text.
- Evaluate, or judge, the piece of writing. Think about what you liked and didn't like and why.

Respond to the Reading

- Talk about the reading with others.
- Discuss the reading in class.
- Write about the reading.
- Create a piece of art or music related to the reading. For example, you might make a poster or write a song lyric.

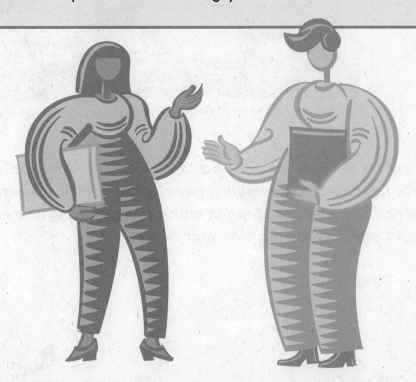

Exercise A Reread "The Father of All Traffic Laws" on pages 66–67. Then reflect on the reading by answering these questions on your own paper.

1. How did things change because of the rules created by William Eno? What does this reading passage teach about the importance of rules?

2. What did you find most interesting in the reading passage? What is your overall opinion of it?

Exercise B Reread "Baking a Good Enough Apple Pie" on pages 71–73. Respond to the reading passage by creating a series of drawings showing the steps in making an apple pie or by writing a short poem about pie. Use your own paper.

Chapter 4

I Think I've Got It!

Reading Comprehension

If you use the active reading strategies described in the previous chapter, you will become a better reader. This chapter will help you to answer questions about what you read. Some reading tests ask about specific details in a passage. However, most questions on reading tests usually ask about one or more of the items listed in this chart:

What to Pay Attention to in Reading Passages

Main Idea: The main point that the author makes

Sequence: The order in which events happen

Causes: The reasons why certain events happen

Effects: What happens as a result of certain events

Vocabulary: The meanings of unfamiliar words in the text

Theme: The lesson, or moral, of the story

Some questions ask about events. Others ask about ideas, such as the main idea of a story or its theme. Still others ask about the meanings of words. If you get in the habit of paying attention to these things as you read, you will spend less time looking back at the text to find the right answers.

Reading Comprehension

Find the Main Idea

Often reading tests ask questions about the main idea. The **main idea** is what the passage is mostly about.

Read the short passage below. Then think about the question that follows it.

There are more than seventy-five kinds of whale. Scientists have divided them into two groups. One group is called the toothed whales. A **toothed whale** hunts fish, squids, and other sea animals for food. The sperm whale is the biggest of all toothed whales. The second group of whales is called the baleen whales. A **baleen whale** scoops up mouthfuls of food and water as it swims. It does not have teeth. Instead, it has long strips, called **baleen,** that hang down from the roof of its mouth. The strips are like a strainer. A row of baleen looks like a great big comb or scrub brush. When a baleen whale gulps a mouthful of water, tiny fish, shrimp, and other small creatures get caught in the baleen. The whale pushes the water out with its tongue and swallows its catch. The blue whale is a baleen whale. It is the biggest animal ever to have lived on Earth.

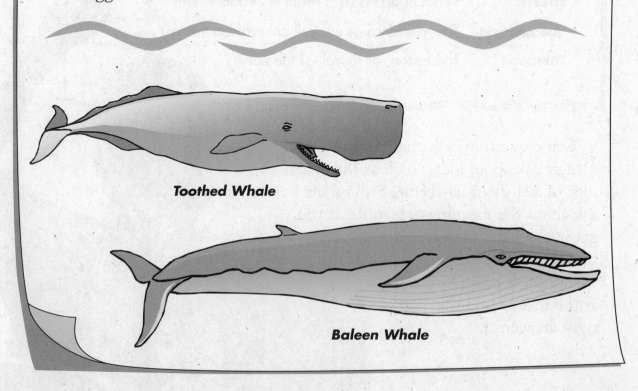

Toothed Whale

Baleen Whale

Think about this question:

What is the main idea of this paragraph?

Ⓐ Baleen whales strain food from the water.

Ⓑ There are two groups of whales: toothed whales and baleen whales.

Ⓒ Toothed whales hunt for food.

Ⓓ The blue whale is the biggest animal ever to have lived on Earth.

ANSWER: Statements A, B, C, and D are all true. However, answers A, C, and D tell about only part of the passage. The main idea is what the reading is *mostly* about. Choose the answer that tells what the passage as a whole is mostly about. Choice B describes the paragraph as a whole. Therefore, choice B is the correct answer.

Sometimes questions that ask about the main idea are written in other ways. Here are some examples:

Questions about the Main Idea

• What is this passage mostly about?

• What would be a good title for this reading passage?

• Which sentence best sums up the passage?

Even though these questions are written in different ways, they all ask about the main idea.

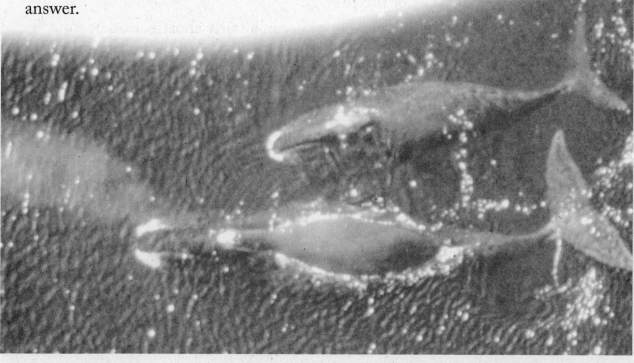

Your Turn

Exercise *Read the short passages below and answer the questions that follow them. Fill in the circle next to the correct answer to each question.*

The first snowboard was invented in the United States in the 1960s. It was called a snurfer. The snurfer was a board with a rope handle attached to its tip. The first snurfers did not have foot straps, or bindings. Riders did not have much control over the board. They could not snurf very far downhill before falling off. Many riders of snurfers were also surfers and skateboarders. Some riders began to experiment with different ways to make snurfers faster and easier to control. Foot bindings were added. By the late 1970s, snurfing, now called snowboarding, was a popular sport. In 1981, the first snowboarding championships were held in the United States. Snowboarding became an Olympic event in 1998 at the Winter Games in Nagano, Japan.

1. What is this passage MOSTLY about?
    Ⓐ how snurfers were invented
    Ⓑ the dangers of early snurfing
    Ⓒ the history of the sport of snowboarding
    Ⓓ why snowboarding is an Olympic event

2. What is the main idea of the passage?
    Ⓐ Snowboarding has come a long way in a fairly short period of time.
    Ⓑ Snowboarding is now the most exciting sport in the Winter Olympics.
    Ⓒ By the late 1970s, snowboarding had become a very popular sport.
    Ⓓ If you can surf or skateboard, then you will probably be good at snowboarding.

Did you know that two-thirds (2/3) of your body is made up of water? Suppose that you weigh 60 pounds. More than 40 pounds of your weight is water. Here is how you can see some of the water that is in your body. First, get a small mirror and hold it close to your mouth. Open your mouth as wide as you can and blow out. Do you see a foggy spot on the mirror? If you touch it, it will feel wet. The spot contains water. The water comes from your breath.

3. A good title for this passage would be
   Ⓐ "Clean Drinking Water."
   Ⓑ "Water Experiments."
   Ⓒ "Two-thirds Water."
   Ⓓ "All About Water."

4. What is the main idea of this passage?
   Ⓐ If you breathe on a mirror, the water in your breath makes a foggy spot.
   Ⓑ The more you weigh, the more water you have in your body.
   Ⓒ Everyone should drink plenty of water each day.
   Ⓓ Our bodies are mostly made up of water.

More ▶

There are more than 120,000 different kinds of ant, bee, and wasp. Ants, bees, and wasps are all insects. They are the only insects with stingers. Ants live together in large groups called colonies. Some bees and wasps also live in colonies, but most live alone. Ants, bees, and wasps all have very strong jaws. They use these jaws to bite and chew. Ants eat both plants and animals. Bees feed on nectar, the sweet liquid from flowers. Wasps eat mainly spiders, insects, and other tiny animals.

5. This passage is MOSTLY about
   (A) what an insect is.
   (B) different types of ant.
   (C) ants, bees, and wasps.
   (D) insects that live in colonies.

6. Which sentence best sums up this passage?
   (A) Insects use their jaws to bite and chew.
   (B) Ants, bees, and wasps are insects that are similar in some ways and different in others.
   (C) Ants, bees, and wasps all live in large groups called colonies.
   (D) Bees eat plants only, and wasps eat animals only, but ants eat plants and animals.

Reading Comprehension

Figure Out the Sequence

Some test questions ask about the sequence of events. An **event** is something that happens. A **sequence** is the order in which events happen.

Read this short passage. Then think about the question below.

> The blimp, also called the airship, was invented in France in 1852. The largest airship ever built was the *Hindenburg*. It was as long as three football fields. The *Hindenburg* carried passengers across the Atlantic Ocean. The *Hindenburg* caught fire and crashed in 1937 while it was preparing to land in Lakehurst, New Jersey. In the second World War, Navy blimps scouted for enemy submarines. Today, scientists use blimps to track whales, to watch oil fields, and to study the atmosphere.

Think about this question:
Which happened LAST?

Ⓐ The *Hindenburg* crashed in New Jersey.

Ⓑ Scientists use blimps to study the atmosphere.

Ⓒ The airship was invented in 1852.

Ⓓ Blimps scouted for enemy submarines during the second World War.

ANSWER: The correct answer is B, "Scientists use blimps to study the atmosphere."

Here are some tips to help you answer sequence questions:

Sequence Clues

1. Pay attention to words like *first, next, then, before, after,* and *finally.* These words tell you when things happened.

2. Always pay attention to dates and times in your reading.

3. Remember that an author usually, but not always, tells the events in the order in which they happened.

Exercise *Read each passage. Then answer the questions that follow it. Fill in the circle next to the correct answer to each question.*

Mount Vesuvius, in Italy, seems like a peaceful mountain with olive trees and grazing animals. Two thousand years ago, one of the worst disasters ever happened there. One afternoon, Mount Vesuvius erupted. The volcano sent out huge clouds of steam, ash, and gas. The ash fell on the town of Pompeii, about six miles away. The villagers fled in fear. Within hours, ash and mud had buried all but the tallest buildings. Pompeii, a once-busy town, vanished!

1. Which of these events happened FIRST?
   Ⓐ A tidal wave hit the town of Pompeii.
   Ⓑ Volcanic ash buried the town of Pompeii.
   Ⓒ Mount Vesuvius erupted.
   Ⓓ Villagers fled in fear.

2. Which of these events happened LAST?
   Ⓐ A tidal wave hit the town of Pompeii.
   Ⓑ Volcanic ash buried the town of Pompeii.
   Ⓒ Mount Vesuvius erupted.
   Ⓓ Villagers fled in fear.

The Fox and the Crow
Based on a fable by Æsop

One day, Fox was walking through the woods, looking for something to eat. He was very hungry. Suddenly, he spotted Crow, high up in the branches of a tree, holding a piece of meat in her beak.

"Morning, Crow," Fox said politely. "I see you have stolen a piece of meat from Man. How clever! Tell me, how did you do it?"

Crow looked down at Fox but did not reply.

"Yes," Fox continued. "Man would have wasted that meat on his dog. But you are so fast, such a great flyer. No wonder you were able to steal that meat."

Still, Crow said nothing. But Fox did not give up.

"Your feathers are very shiny today, Crow—beautiful. Almost as beautiful as your singing! If you could sing just one song . . ."

Crow let out a long screech and dropped her prize to the ground. Quickly, Fox grabbed the meat.

"Thanks for the meat, Crow. Your screeching is beautiful because it is my breakfast bell!"

Moral: Watch out for false praise. O

3. Which of these events happened FIRST?
   Ⓐ Fox told Crow she was a great flyer.
   Ⓑ Fox spotted Crow in the branches of a tree.
   Ⓒ Crow dropped the meat to the ground.
   Ⓓ Fox asked Crow to sing a song.

Reading Comprehension

Look for Causes and Effects

Sometimes, one event **causes** another to happen. For example, putting bread in a toaster can cause it to turn crispy and brown. Getting a good grade is an effect of doing your homework. Patting a dog can cause its tail to wag. When one event makes a second one happen, the second event is called an **effect**.

CAUSE	EFFECT
Putting bread in a toaster ——→	Bread turns crispy and brown.
Patting a dog ——————→	The dog wags its tail.
Doing your homework ——————→	You get a good grade.

Writers often describe causes and effects. Read this short passage. Then think about the questions that follow it.

The Nile crocodile has a tough, scaly hide. Because the hide can be used for shoes, belts, and handbags, people hunt the crocodile. In Egypt, too much hunting almost made the crocodile disappear. So in 1984, the Egyptian government banned crocodile hunting. Once they were protected, Nile crocodiles began to do well in the warm waters of Lake Nasser in southern Egypt. Today, as many as ten thousand crocodiles live in the lake.

Think about this question:
What caused the Nile crocodile almost to disappear?
- Ⓐ its tough, scaly hide
- Ⓑ too much hunting
- Ⓒ too little food
- Ⓓ the warm waters of Lake Nasser

ANSWER: The correct answer to this question is choice B. The passage does say that the crocodile's tough hide can be used for shoes, belts, and handbags. But it says that too much hunting is what *caused* the crocodile almost to be wiped out.

Think about this question:

How did the Egyptian government protect the Nile crocodile?

Ⓐ It moved crocodiles from the Nile River to Lake Nasser.

Ⓑ It used cow hide instead of crocodile hide to make shoes.

Ⓒ It banned crocodile hunting.

Ⓓ It banned the sale of crocodile handbags.

ANSWER: The correct answer to this question is choice C. The text doesn't say anything about using cow hide to make shoes. It does not say anything about making it against the law to sell crocodile handbags. The text also says nothing about moving crocodiles from the Nile to Lake Nasser. The passage does say that the Egyptian government protected the Nile crocodile by banning crocodile hunting.

Notice that questions about causes and effects do not have to have the word *cause* or the word *effect* in them. Any question asking about one event that makes another event happen is a cause-and-effect question.

CAUSE	EFFECT
There is too much crocodile hunting. →	The crocodile almost disappears.
The hunting of crocodile is banned. →	There are more crocodiles.

Exercise *Read each passage. Then answer the questions that follow it. Fill in the circle next to the correct answer to each question.*

Around Antarctica, the ocean is sometimes covered by a lid of ice. The ice spreads or shrinks depending on the season. When the short summer ends, ice crystals form on the sea and make it look greasy. As the water becomes colder, this greasy-looking ice thickens into bigger pieces, often shaped like circles or pancakes. The pieces of floating ice bump into each other in the waves, eventually building big blocks of ice called ice floes. When ice floes pile up on each other, they can make a sheet of pack ice up to sixteen feet thick! In the summer, the pack ice melts and breaks up.

1. How do ice floes form?
   - Ⓐ Greasy-looking ice thickens into bigger pieces that bump into each other.
   - Ⓑ Melting pack ice runs into the sea.
   - Ⓒ People create the ice floes.
   - Ⓓ Warm summers cause ice floes.

2. When the summer comes to Antarctica,
   - Ⓐ ice crystals form on the sea.
   - Ⓑ pack ice melts and breaks up.
   - Ⓒ polar bears hibernate.
   - Ⓓ ice floes form.

As Diego climbed into his small, red pickup truck, he noticed that the sky had become very dark. He turned the key, trying to ignore his uneasy feelings. A big drop of rain fell on the windshield, then another, and another. Driving slowly, he ignored the loud horn of a large car close behind him. Soon, it was raining so hard that Diego could barely see. He turned on the windshield wipers as fast as they could go. Too late, he saw the bull in the middle of the road. He slammed on the brakes and felt the truck spinning wildly on the slippery road. He stopped just in time to see the bull run into the meadow.

3. Which of the following did NOT cause Diego's truck to spin in the road?
   Ⓐ It was raining so hard that Diego could barely see.
   Ⓑ There was a car behind him.
   Ⓒ The road was slippery.
   Ⓓ He slammed on the brakes.

4. All of the following effects were caused by the heavy rain EXCEPT which one?
   Ⓐ The bull was standing in the middle of the road.
   Ⓑ Diego turned on the windshield wipers as fast as they could go.
   Ⓒ The road became slippery.
   Ⓓ Diego could barely see.

Look for Context Clues

Sometimes when you are reading, you come to a word that you do not know. Often you can figure out the meaning of the word by looking at the words that come before and after it. We call this way of understanding a word looking at the word in **context.** To help you figure out the meaning of the word, you can find hints in the writing around the word. These hints are called **context clues.**

Read this short passage carefully. Then see if you can use context clues to guess the meaning of the words in **boldface** type.

Many insects and animals have colors and patterns that help to protect them against **predators** that might eat them. **Camouflage** also helps predators to hunt. Grasshoppers and tree snakes are green. They match the grass and leaves around them, which makes them hard to see. Polar bears live in the Arctic and are white. The color of their fur helps them to blend into the snow and ice as they search for food.

Sometimes, if there are no context clues for figuring out a word's meaning, you can figure out the meaning from **word parts.** For example, *disassembled = dis + assembled.* Since *dis–* means "not," you know that *disassembled* means "not assembled or put together." See pages 77–81 for more information on using word parts.

Think about this question:
What is *camouflage*?

Ⓐ bright colors that warn away enemies

Ⓑ loud, frightening noises that animals make

Ⓒ stinging or biting

Ⓓ colors or patterns that look like the surroundings

ANSWER: The descriptions of the insects and animals give you clues about what *camouflage* means. Grasshoppers and tree snakes are green, and polar bears are white. These are not warning colors, so choice A is not the answer. The passage does not state anything about animals or insects making loud noises, so B is not a good answer. Though insects can bite or sting and animals can bite, again, there is no mention of this in the passage. The passage points out that grasshoppers and tree snakes are the color of grass and leaves, and that polar bears are the color of snow and ice. The best answer is choice D, "colors or patterns that look like the surroundings."

Now think about this question:
What is a *predator*?

Ⓐ an animal that hides from its enemies

Ⓑ an animal that hunts for and eats other animals

Ⓒ an animal that eats grass and leaves

Ⓓ an animal that lives in trees

ANSWER: If you scan for the word *predators*, you will see that it is followed by the words "that might eat them" and surrounded by the words "helps (them) to hunt." These are two context clues that tell you what a predator does: It hunts other animals and eats them. Although some predators might live in trees or hide from their enemies, the best answer is choice C, "an animal that hunts for and eats other animals."

Exercise *Read the short passages on these two pages and use context clues to answer the questions that follow each passage. Fill in the circle next to the correct answer to each question.*

A Mrs. Sneed was a **perfectionist.** She could not stand anything out of place. She walked around the house with a broom in her hand, and if she saw a crumb on the floor, she pounced on it. She cleared away the newspaper while Mr. Sneed was still reading it. She even slept neatly. When she awoke, her covers were tucked in, and her pillow was barely wrinkled.

1. The passage above describes what kind of person Mrs. Sneed is. Using context clues, you can figure out that the word *perfectionist* means
   Ⓐ someone who is snobby.
   Ⓑ someone who acts nervous.
   Ⓒ someone who wants everything to be just right.
   Ⓓ someone who is very active.

B The mayor and other **notables** of Francestown led the Fourth of July parade. Riding in a Model T car was the oldest person in town, 99-year-old Mildred Chapman. The police chief and the fire chief followed on foot.

2. The parade was led by the mayor and other notables. What is a *notable*?
   Ⓐ someone who take notes
   Ⓑ anyone in uniform
   Ⓒ a person who is important
   Ⓓ someone who knows a lot

C   **Stealthily,** like a thief in the night, Manuel crept up silently behind Big Al, who was snoring loudly on the porch rocker. Without a sound, he lifted up the bucket of ice-cold water and swiftly dumped it on top of Big Al's head.

3. Stealthily, like a thief in the night, Manuel crept up behind Big Al. What does *stealthily* mean?
    - (A) noisily
    - (B) very quietly
    - (C) angrily
    - (D) fearfully

D   As Mr. Plum looked up from the letter he was reading, a look of complete surprise crossed his face. Shaking his head in wonder, Mr. Plum quickly stuffed the letter back in its envelope. He opened and closed his mouth, trying to say something. For once, the chatty Mr. Plum was completely **dumbfounded.**

4. For once, Mr. Plum was completely dumbfounded. What does *dumbfounded* mean?
    - (A) fooled
    - (B) stupid
    - (C) speechless
    - (D) delighted

E   The early morning peace was broken only by the cry of a loon, swimming far out in the middle of the lake. Simon looked over the **placid** water, sparkling in the sunlight. Not a single ripple upset its smooth surface.

5. Simon looked over the placid water. What does *placid* mean?
    - (A) deep
    - (B) icy
    - (C) dark blue
    - (D) calm

Find the Theme

At the beginning of this chapter, you learned about main ideas. A main idea is an important point that a writer makes. A main idea in a story is also called a theme.

Usually, the **theme** of a story is a lesson that the story teaches. Often, this is a lesson learned by the main character.

Read the very short story below and the question that follows it.

The Team Player
by Maude Chapman

It was a perfect day for the first baseball practice of the season. The sky was a bright blue, and a soft breeze was blowing. Joe and Sophie tossed a ball back and forth. The coach checked off names as players showed up.

"Oh, great," Joe groaned. "Look who's on our team."

Sophie looked where Joe was pointing. She saw Sam Baker grab a bat, helmet, and glove from the back of a car. He was wearing their team's red T-shirt. It seemed much too large for him.

"Well," Sophie asked Joe, "what's wrong with Sam?"

"Just look at him!" Joe exclaimed. "He's small—too small! He'll never hit the ball out of the infield—that is, if he *can* hit the ball at all. And who knows if he can catch or throw?"

Sophie said, "Don't be so quick to judge. Remember what you said about me, when I showed up for my first practice?"

Joe's face turned a deep pink. Sophie was one of the best players on the Cardinals now. She played shortstop and never seemed to miss a ball. She had a strong arm and was a great hitter. Joe had a lot of respect for her as a player now. When she had walked onto the field her first day, however, Joe had complained loudly.

"A *girl??*" he had said. "Great! We might as well pack up and go home. We'll never win any games with a *girl* on the team!" Later, he was proven wrong. He and Sophie became friends.

Soon Joe saw that he was wrong about Sam, too. Joe watched in surprise as Sam dove for the ball, catching it in his glove every time. At batting practice, Sam hit a fast grounder up the third base line. Running hard, Sam rounded first base with lightning speed.

He was so fast that the throw to second came well after he was safely on base.

"Think we might win a few games after all, even with Sam on the team?" Sophie teased Joe.

Joe looked at his feet.

"I guess you're right, Sophie," Joe replied. "I shouldn't have judged Sam without seeing him play. Size isn't everything." ○

Think about this question:
Which of the following sentences states the lesson in this story?

Ⓐ Everything is beautiful in its own way.

Ⓑ Practice makes perfect.

Ⓒ Look before you leap.

Ⓓ Don't judge a person before you see what he or she can do.

ANSWER: Choice D is the answer that best describes the lesson that Joe learns.

A **fable** is a story with animal characters. It is told to teach a lesson. The lesson is called a **moral.** Questions that ask about the moral of a fable or the lesson in a story are **theme questions.**

Exercise Read the stories on these two pages. Then answer the questions that follow the stories. Fill in the circle next to the correct answer to each question.

A The Rabbit and the Turtle

Rabbit sat by the side of the road and watched Turtle slowly creep by.

"Look out! Don't crash into anything," Rabbit teased.

"You might be fast," Turtle said, "but I could beat you in a race." Rabbit thought a race might be good for a laugh. They set the day for the race and asked Fox to help.

Fox called out, "Begin!" Rabbit and Turtle started off together. Rabbit soon left Turtle behind. Turtle did not give up. He just put one foot in front of the other.

Rabbit said, "I will play a joke on Turtle. I will lie by the side of the road and let Turtle pass me. Then I will dash by him."

Rabbit waited and waited. Finally, he fell asleep in the sun. When he woke up, he saw Turtle and Fox resting on the other side of the finish line.

1. Which saying BEST expresses the lesson, or moral, of this fable?
- Ⓐ Experience is the best teacher.
- Ⓑ Mother knows best.
- Ⓒ Slow and steady wins the race.
- Ⓓ The first step is the hardest.

B Valentine Surprise
by Carmel Jackson

On the Friday before Valentine's Day, the Kids Care Club at my school met to make valentine cards. We cut out hearts, glued them onto doilies, and decorated them with glitter, stickers, and ribbon. Then, after school on Valentine's Day, we went to deliver our cards at the Wedgewood Nursing Home.

I had fun making the valentines, but I wasn't sure I wanted to go to the nursing home. The people were so old—one was a great-great-grandma! Some of them were hard to understand, and they were all so wrinkly.

At first, we were a little shy, but then we started to pass out valentines and shake people's hands. It really was pretty easy! The people all smiled and said "thank you" a hundred times. Some had candy to give to us. One man, Mr. Nichols, played two games of checkers with me. He beat me both times, but I learned some new moves.

It was fun going to the nursing home, and it made me feel good inside. Giving valentines to the people there was better than getting presents myself. Next time, I am going to ask my friends if they would like to come, too.

2. What is a lesson that the writer of this piece wants the readers to learn?
   - Ⓐ Doing nice things for others can make a person feel good.
   - Ⓑ When people get old, they slow down.
   - Ⓒ Making presents is better than buying them.
   - Ⓓ Children can't understand older people.

3. What saying BEST expresses the theme of this story?
   - Ⓐ Don't give presents to strangers.
   - Ⓑ It is better to give than to receive.
   - Ⓒ Don't look a gift horse in the mouth.
   - Ⓓ Never put off until tomorrow what you can do today.

Reading Comprehension

Reading Strategies Review

1. Scan the parts to find the main idea.

These kinds of questions are asking about the main idea:

"What is this story about?"
"What would be a good title for this story?"

Scan the parts of the story to see if you can find what the whole story is about.

2. Scan to find details.

To find a detail or specific fact or description, find the **key words** in the questions first. Then scan the text, looking for those key words. When you find them, stop and read slowly for the answer(s) you need.

3. Figure out the sequence.

Look for words that tell when things take place. Words like *first*, *next*, *then*, *before*, *after*, and *finally* tell when events happened. Watch for dates and times.

4. Look for causes and effects.

Watch for words like *because*, *cause*, *therefore*, *result*, *effect*, and *so*. These words show causes and effects. When an event makes something happen, the event is the **cause** and the result is the **effect.**

5. Look for context clues to figure out meaning.

When you come across a word that you do not know, try to guess its meaning based on the words around it. Look for context clues in the words around the unfamiliar word. Sometimes the author tells the meaning of hard words in the story. Sometimes, the other parts of the story will give clues to the meaning of a word.

6. Find the theme.

Look for a lesson that the story teaches. Most important is any lesson that the main character learns.

7. Pick the best answer to each question.

First, look for answers that are clearly wrong.
Choose the **best** answer from those that are left.

Return to the exercises at the beginning of the unit. Check your work and fix it if necessary. Give the exercises to your teacher for grading.

Unit 3
A World of Good Reading

Read the following passages. The first passage is a true story. The second one is a poem. Answer the questions that follow the reading passages. At the end of the unit, you will be asked to come back to these questions to check your work and correct it if necessary.

Mr. Handyman

by Jackie Starr

One Saturday morning at the end of the summer of 1935, Don got up. He could not turn the doorknob with his right hand. His mother said that he must have slept on his arm. He felt fine, so he went off to play with a friend.

At dinner the next day, he began to feel sick. His parents called the doctor. The doctor thought that Don might have polio. **Polio** is a sickness that makes moving (and sometimes even breathing) very difficult. Don's parents took him to the hospital. Polio can spread from one person to another, so Don was put into a room alone. He had to be kept away from other people so they would not get sick. Only the doctors and nurses could come near him. Everyone who came into the room had to wear a mask and gown. Their clothes had to be washed as soon as they left the room.

Today, babies and young children are given a special medicine called a **vaccine.** The vaccine protects people against polio. When Don was a boy, however, there was no polio vaccine.

Don's right arm got weaker. Soon, he could not straighten it at all. A special brace was made for his arm. It held his arm straight out from the side of his body. He wore the brace day and night for the next two years. He took it off only to take baths.

The brace was one of Don's trickiest problems. The brace was very heavy and stiff. It made it hard for him to move around. He could not even roll over in bed. Don had to find different ways to do everyday tasks.

Don could not go to school at all that year. A teacher came to his house to help him learn. When he finished his work, he and the teacher played board games.

Don was right-handed. He had to learn to do things all over again with his left hand. He learned to write "lefty." He could even tie knots with the help of his feet.

Don liked to build radios. He worked on them with only his left hand at first. When Don's brace came off, his right arm was small and weak. Still, he learned to use that arm and hand again.

Don's interest in radios and electricity grew. He learned more about how things work and how to fix them when they didn't work. He built and fixed radios. He worked on radio-controlled toy airplanes. He even worked at a radio store and at a radio station.

In college, Don studied to become an engineer. **Engineers** design and build things. For forty years, Don has used his skills in many ways to build and fix things for people.

Don's children always knew that he could fix anything. They brought broken toys, dolls, and gadgets to their father to be fixed. Now Don's grandchildren bring their broken toys to him. They know that Grandpa will find a way to fix them. ○

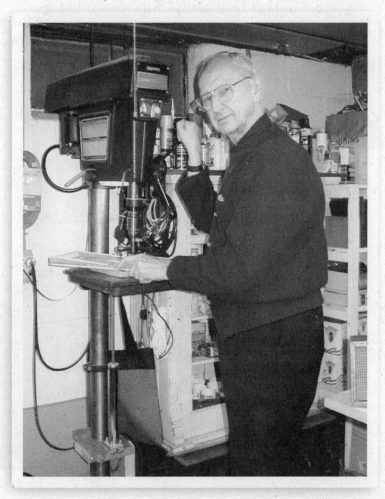

Thanks to Dad
by Sterling Moore

When I was a young boy, playing with my dad,
I stumbled and took a big fall.
He said, "Hop up, brush off your knees, Lad,
And keep running with the ball."

When my racehorse threw me, while jumping a fence,
And broke my leg in three places,
My dad said, "As soon as you walk again, Son,
You must remount and rejoin the races."

When I asked lovely Carolyn Jean to the dance,
And she broke my heart with her "No,"
I would've stayed home to mope and moan
But Dad said, "Son, you must go."

Now, thanks to Dad, when life throws me punches,
I know how to take them in stride.
I brush myself off, remount and go on,
Knowing he would be grinning with pride. o

Your Turn

Exercise *Fill in the circle next to the correct answer to each question.*

1. What is the story MOSTLY about?
   Ⓐ Polio is a serious disease that can be prevented by a vaccine.
   Ⓑ Don's grandchildren bring him toys to be fixed.
   Ⓒ Engineers design and build many things.
   Ⓓ Don learned how to build and fix things even though he had a weak arm.

2. What was the FIRST sign that something was wrong with Don?
   Ⓐ He felt sick.
   Ⓑ He couldn't turn a doorknob.
   Ⓒ His arm would not move.
   Ⓓ He had a fever.

3. What did Don learn to do after he came home from the hospital?
   Ⓐ He learned to read.
   Ⓑ He learned to walk again.
   Ⓒ He learned how to do things with his left hand.
   Ⓓ He learned how to fly airplanes.

4. The story mentions all the jobs listed below EXCEPT
   Ⓐ working at a radio station.
   Ⓑ working as an engineer.
   Ⓒ working as a train conductor.
   Ⓓ working at a radio store.

5. By the end of the story, Don has become
   Ⓐ a doctor.
   Ⓑ a grandfather.
   Ⓒ a pilot.
   Ⓓ the president of a company.

More ▶

6. Which of the following words BEST describes Don?
   - A determined
   - B sad
   - C lonely
   - D funny

7. Which of the following BEST describes the speaker in the poem?
   - A a man who is thinking about the important lessons his father taught him
   - B a father who is thinking about the important lessons he wants to teach his son
   - C a boy who is thinking about the things he would like to do when he grows up
   - D a boy who is thinking of the things he could do to make his father proud

8. Which of the following is NOT something the speaker of the poem describes?
   - A getting into a fist fight
   - B falling off a horse
   - C falling down playing ball
   - D asking a girl to a dance

9. The speaker believes that his dad will be "grinning with pride" whenever he (the speaker)
   - A makes a touchdown.
   - B thinks about memories from his childhood.
   - C wins a horse race.
   - D overcomes a setback and carries on.

10. Compare Don in the story with the speaker in the poem. In what ways are the two characters similar? Use details from the story and the poem in your answer.

_____

_____

_____

_____

_____

_____

Chapter 5

Truth Be Told

Understanding Nonfiction

Think about all the types of reading that you do in various subject areas in school. You probably have a science textbook and a math textbook. In language arts, you probably read stories and poetry. You might have noticed that the way you read a story for language arts is different from the way that you read a chapter in a math textbook. If so, you have already learned one of the main rules of reading: *Do not read every piece of writing in the same way.*

In this chapter and the two that follow, you will learn about some of the main types of reading passage that you will come across in school

and on reading tests. Learning what to look for in passages of different types will help you to get more from your reading.

What Is Nonfiction?

The type of writing that you probably read most often is nonfiction. **Nonfiction** is writing that tells about real people and events. Some examples of nonfiction include textbooks, biographies, magazine articles, book reviews, encyclopedia articles, speeches, essays, and reports.

When you read a piece of nonfiction writing, here are some important features you should notice:

Features of Nonfiction

Subject   The **subject** is what the piece as a whole is about.

Thesis   The **thesis** is the main idea, or point, of the piece.

Purpose   The **purpose** is what the writer wants to accomplish (i.e., to tell a story, describe something, persuade the reader, or present information).

Organization   The **organization** is the way the writer arranges his or her information.

Subject and Thesis

The **subject** of a piece of writing is what the piece as a whole is about. For example, in the opening pages of this unit, you read a piece of nonfiction called "Mr. Handyman." The subject of this reading passage is Don, a boy who got polio. The **thesis** of a piece of nonfiction writing is the main idea or point that the writer makes about the subject. In "Mr. Handyman," the thesis is that Don was able to overcome his disabilities with hard work and determination. In some types of nonfiction, the thesis will be stated in a single sentence called the **thesis statement.** The thesis statement can usually be found near the beginning of the text.

Purpose

The **purpose** of a piece of writing is the reason that the writer wrote the piece. There are four main purposes for writing:

- to narrate, or tell a story
- to describe something
- to persuade, or convince readers to believe something or do something
- to inform readers about a topic

Types of Writing

Narrative writing tells a story. Narrative nonfiction includes biographies and autobiographies, stories about real people and events.

Descriptive writing describes a subject. This type of writing does not usually appear by itself. It is commonly used in other types of writing. For example, a narrative might include a paragraph that describes the setting or a character in the story.

Persuasive writing tries to convince the reader to agree with an opinion or to take some kind of action. For example, when a candidate gives a campaign speech, she is trying to persuade the audience to vote for her.

Informative writing presents information. A textbook is an example of informative writing. Its purpose is to provide you with information.

As you scan a reading passage, try to figure out its purpose. You will be able to tell right away if the passage is a story (narrative writing) or a description. In this chapter, you will learn what to look for when the narrative or description is about real people and events. Later in this unit, you will learn what to look for when you read fictional narratives about imaginary people and events.

It may be difficult at times to tell the difference between informative and persuasive writing. Persuasive writing also provides information, so it seems similar to informative writing. There is one main difference between these two types of writing: Informative writing simply presents facts. Persuasive writing presents facts in order to convince you to do or believe something.

A **fact** is a statement that can be proved to be true. You can look it up, or you can tell it is true by testing it yourself. An **opinion** is a statement that one or more people believe but with which others may disagree.

Notice the difference in the pairs of statements below. One statement in each pair is a fact. The other is an opinion.

FACT: Tulip bulbs should be planted in the early spring or fall. *(This is a fact that can be looked up in a gardening book. If you plant tulip bulbs at other times of the year, they will not flower.)*

OPINION: Tulips are the nicest of all the bulb plants. *(This is the writer's opinion. Others may think that daffodils or crocuses are the nicest bulb plants.)*

FACT: Loud noises can damage the inner ear. *(This is a fact that can be looked up in a medical reference book.)*

OPINION: Children should never wear headphones. *(This is the writer's opinion. Others may argue that children can wear headphones, as long as they keep the volume at a low level.)*

Informative writing may contain sections that look like other forms of writing. For example, an article that informs you about baking bread might contain description. It might tell what the bread smells like. The article might also contain persuasion. It might try to convince you to bake your own bread instead of buying it at the store.

Some types of informative writing should contain facts only, with no opinions. A history text should just give facts. A news story should also include facts only. In a newspaper, opinions should be found only on the editorial page, in the letters to the editor, and in advertisements.

Your Turn

Exercise A *Read each paragraph below and answer the questions that follow. Remember that some writing has more than one purpose.*

I will always remember Ms. Hanegan's fourth-grade spelling bee as one of the worst days I've ever had. I was sure that I would do well in the spelling bee. After all, I always got good grades on my weekly spelling tests. So, as all my friends studied extra hard for the spelling bee, I played with my little brother and did everything else but study. The night before the spelling bee, I got a little nervous and started to study, but I didn't have time to do much before I had to go to bed. The next day, I made it through the first two rounds. Then I got the word *Mississippi*. I misspelled it and was out of the competition. I was so embarrassed! Later my friend told me that *Mississippi* was on the review sheet. If I had only studied, I would have known how to spell it. I may have lost the spelling bee, but I learned an important lesson that day about being prepared, and I've never forgotten it.

1. What is the purpose of this paragraph?

   _____

2. Explain how you can tell.

   _____

   _____

   _____

There are many unusual types of snake in the world, but the king cobra is truly one of a kind. It is actually not a cobra at all but is in a genus of its very own. King cobras grow to be much longer than true cobras, reaching lengths of up to eighteen feet. When a king cobra is angry, it will spread its hood and raise its head nearly six feet in the air. Imagine what a scary sight that would be! Perhaps that is why adult king cobras have no natural enemies. Another big difference between king cobras and other cobras is that king cobras make a nest for their young. In fact, they are the only snakes in the world known to do this. Some believe this is a sign of the king cobra's remarkable intelligence.

3. What is the purpose of this paragraph?

_____

4. Explain how you can tell.

_____

_____

_____

If you like hamburgers that taste as if they've been cooked on the grill in your backyard, then it's time to try Bob's Backyard Burgers. We use only the finest ingredients and cook our hamburgers over a real grill, so they taste just like they're homemade. You can't beat our prices. Come on down for the best burger in town.

5. What is the purpose of this paragraph?

_____

6. Explain how you can tell.

_____

_____

_____

More ▶

Your Turn

Exercise B *Below is a newspaper story written by a young reporter. This reporter made the mistake of including some opinions in the story. Find the sentences or phrases (groups of words) that state opinions. Then draw a line through them so that the news story gives only facts.*

A New Baby at the Zoo

MAY 14 There is a new baby at the Zenith Park Zoo. On Tuesday, Geraldine the giraffe gave birth to Tawny.

Geraldine is six years old. She is the sweetest animal at the zoo. Tawny is her first calf. Geraldine stays right by her calf at all times. She is such a devoted mother!

By Saturday, groups were allowed to visit the newborn. Tawny hid behind her mother like a shy child. Tawny's legs are skinny and ugly. Geraldine stretched her neck to grab the leaves above her with her 18-inch tongue. Tawny will drink milk from her mother for at least a year.

In the wild, lions or hyenas kill most giraffe calves in their first months of life. Zoos, on the other hand, allow giraffes to breed and care for their young in complete safety. Tawny must be glad to be in such a safe place.

Organization

A good writer organizes his or her ideas and information in a logical way. Good organization helps the reader figure out what information is important.

The following chart describes some typical methods of organization used by writers:

Methods of Organization

Chronological Order (Time Order)	A writer presents events in the order in which they occurred. This method is often used in narrative writing (stories). The story begins at a certain point in time, and the events are described in order as they happen.
Spatial Order	A writer presents details in order of appearance, such as from left to right, from top to bottom, or from near to far. This method is often used in descriptive writing.
Cause-and-Effect Order	A writer presents a **cause,** an event that makes something else happen. Then the writer describes the **effect,** the thing that happens as a result of the cause. In some cases, a writer might describe the effect first and then explain the causes.
Comparison-and-Contrast Order	A writer talks about the similarities and/or differences among two or more subjects. Sometimes a writer will describe one subject completely and then point out how the second subject is similar to, or different from, the first. Or a writer may compare the subjects point by point.
Degree Order	A writer presents details or ideas in the order of their importance. Usually, a writer will present the most important detail first and then work down to the least important detail.

The method of organization that the writer uses is a major clue about what you should pay attention to as you read. Suppose you come across a reading passage that is organized in cause-and-effect order. You can be sure that it will be important to know the causes and effects described.

Types of Informative Nonfiction

Let's look at three common types of informative nonfiction: 1) writing that explains how to do something, 2) writing that compares and contrasts, and 3) writing that explains causes and effects. For each type of writing, there are certain questions that you should ask yourself as you read.

Writing That Explains a Process

A **process essay** gives directions or explains the steps in a process. The selection on pages 71–73 that explains how to bake an apple pie is an example of this type of writing. The questions below will help you as you read writing that explains how to do something.

Questions to Ask about Writing That Explains a Process

1. What process does this piece explain?

2. What are the steps in this process?

3. Do these steps need to be in a certain order? (If so, make note of the correct order.)

4. Have any important steps been left out?

Writing That Compares and Contrasts

To **compare** is to show how things are alike. To **contrast** is to show how they are different. Writing that compares and contrasts talks about how two or more people, places, or things are alike and different. The paragraph on page 92 that explains how ants, wasps, and bees are alike and different is an example of this type of writing. As you read writing that compares and contrasts, ask yourself questions like those shown in the chart below.

Questions to Ask about Writing That Compares and Contrasts

1. What people, places, or things are being compared and contrasted?
2. How are they alike?
3. How are they different?
4. Are there any important similarities or differences that the writer didn't mention?

Apples and oranges?

Writing That Explains Causes and Effects

In writing that explains causes and effects, a writer might name several causes leading up to an event. The writer might also name several events that were caused by one thing. The paragraph on page 96 about the Nile crocodile is an example of this type of writing.

Just because one event follows another does not mean that one caused the other. Look at these examples:

First you raise your hand.
Then you ask a question.

Raising your hand *did not* cause you to ask a question.

First you raise your hand.
Then the teacher calls on you.

Raising your hand *did* cause the teacher to call on you.

Ask yourself these questions as you read:

Questions to Ask about Writing That Explains Causes and Effects

1. What cause or causes does the writer point out?
2. What are the effects?
3. What facts and examples has the writer included to show that the causes led to the effects?

Your Turn

Exercise *Read each short passage and follow the directions below it.*

Making pizza is not hard. You need some basic ingredients: cornmeal, store-bought pizza dough, olive oil, tomato sauce, mozzarella cheese, and spices. You will also need a pizza pan and an oven. Work with an older member of your family. Follow these simple directions.

First, wash your hands! Next, preheat the oven to 500°F. While the oven is warming up, use cornmeal to powder the pizza pan lightly. This will keep the dough from sticking. Then flatten the ball of dough and spread it in a circle on the pan.

Drizzle olive oil on top of the flat circle of dough. Then spread tomato sauce in a thin layer. Add whatever spices you like. Garlic, pepper, and oregano are good choices. Add the shredded cheese next. Spread the cheese out over the dough so that it melts evenly.

Use potholders or oven mitts to slide the pan into the oven. Bake the pizza in a hot oven for 10 to 15 minutes. Finally, enjoy your tasty creation!

1. What is the purpose of this selection?

   _____

2. Find the questions on pages 124–125 that you should ask about this type of writing and answer them on your own paper.

Many people use the words *crocodile* and *alligator* to mean the same thing. In fact, they are different animals. Do you know the differences between crocodiles and alligators?

Both crocodiles and alligators are reptiles. Like other reptiles, they both have scaly skin, and the females lay eggs. In addition, these two animals are cold-blooded. (Their body temperature gets warmer or cooler depending on their surroundings.) Both alligators and crocodiles live in warm regions and spend most of their time in the water.

Alligators are generally smaller than crocodiles. They have shorter, wider snouts, and their teeth are hidden when their mouths are closed. Crocodiles have long, narrow snouts. The sharp teeth on their lower jaws can be seen clearly, even when their mouths are closed. Crocodiles are muddy brown. Alligators are darker and sometimes look almost black.

3. What is the purpose of this selection?

_____

4. Find the questions on pages 124–125 that you should ask about this type of writing and answer them on your own paper.

More ▶

Have you ever wondered why there are seasons? Why is it cold in the winter and hot in the summer? The answer is simple: It is because the earth is tilted on its axis. Instead of sitting straight up, with the North Pole at its very top and the South Pole at its very bottom, the earth leans to one side. When the North Pole is leaning toward the sun, it is summertime in the northern hemisphere (the top half of the planet). At this time of year, in the part of the planet north of the equator (the imaginary line that runs around the middle of the earth), the days are longer. In addition, the sunlight is much stronger because it hits the earth from almost directly overhead. This results in warm days and nights. As the planet makes its yearly journey around the sun, the North Pole becomes tilted away from the sun. Then it is wintertime in the northern hemisphere. The days are shorter, and the sunlight is weaker because it hits this part of the earth at a sharp angle (not directly overhead). This results in colder days and nights. In the southern hemisphere it is exactly the opposite. When the northern half of the planet is tilted away from the sun, the southern half is tilted toward it. So, when it is winter in the northern hemisphere, it is summer in the southern hemisphere. Countries close to the equator get about the same amount of sunlight at the same angle all year round, so they do not experience seasons like countries north and south of them do.

5. What is the purpose of this selection?

_____

6. Find the questions on pages 124–125 that you should ask about this type of writing and answer them on your own paper.

Understanding Nonfiction

Narrative Nonfiction

All the short passages you just read are examples of informative nonfiction. Their purpose is to provide you with information. Another type of nonfiction is narrative nonfiction. The purpose of **narrative nonfiction** is to tell a story about a real person, event, or place. The first passage that you read in this unit, "Mr. Handyman," is an example of narrative nonfiction. It is a story about a real boy named Don who got polio.

Nonfiction narratives and fictional stories have a lot in common. In both, there are characters. There is a setting, which is where the story takes place. There is a very important difference between nonfiction and fiction stories, though: The events in a nonfiction story actually happened. The characters are real. So are the places. In fiction, the characters and events are made up.

Three types of narrative nonfiction that you will see often are biography, autobiography, and history. This chart can help you tell them apart.

Types of Narrative Nonfiction

Type	Characteristics
Biography	• Tells a story about a person's life • The author is not the main character
Autobiography	• The author tells a story about his or her own life
History	• Tells a story about an interesting event or time • The author usually is not a character in the story

All three types of narrative nonfiction are alike in one way. Most of the time, they tell about events in the same order in which they happened. Biographies and autobiographies are alike because they both tell about a person's life. The difference is that in a biography, the writer tells about someone else's life. In an autobiography, the writer tells about his or her own life. Histories are different from biographies and autobiographies. They usually focus on events that happened to more than one person in the past, instead of on one person's life.

Here are some things you should notice as you read narrative nonfiction:

Features of Narrative Nonfiction

Characters   The **characters** are the people in the story. Often there is one main character. Ask yourself why the writer chose to write about this person. What does the writer want you to learn from this person's experience?

Setting   The **setting** is the place where the story happens and the time period. Ask yourself if there is anything unusual about the setting. Is the setting especially important to the story?

Events   The **events** are what happens in the story. In nonfiction narratives, the writer picks and chooses events from the main character's life to tell you about. Ask yourself why the writer chose these events to describe.

Theme   The **theme** is the message of the story. Think about how the story made you feel. What lesson did you learn from this story? Think about what the writer says about the main character. What events did the writer choose to include? These can help you to figure out the message the writer is trying to get across.

Your Turn

Exercise *Read the short nonfiction narrative below. Then answer the questions that follow. Write your answers in complete sentences.*

Helen Keller was born in 1880 in Alabama. She was two years old when she became ill. She had a high fever that left her deaf, blind, and unable to speak. Her world was silent and dark. To get what she wanted, Helen kicked and screamed. Helen's world changed when a teacher named Annie Sullivan came to live at her house. Annie used sign language to spell out words in Helen's hand. Helen quickly learned how to spell words, but she did not understand what the words meant. One day, Annie placed Helen's hand under a water pump. Annie spelled out "w-a-t-e-r" over and over in Helen's other hand. Suddenly, Helen understood that those letters meant the wet liquid she was feeling. She began to touch everything around her, asking Annie for their names. Later, Helen

Keller learned to read and write using raised dots on paper. This way of reading and writing is called Braille. She also learned to speak. When she grew up, she went to college. She wrote books. She also traveled the world speaking about blindness. She became a role model for all people trying to overcome difficulties. ○

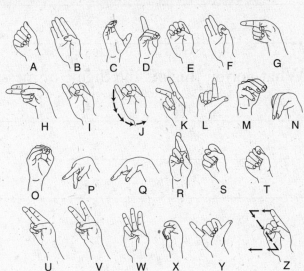

More ▶

1. What type of narrative nonfiction is this passage—a biography, an autobiography, or a history?

   _____

2. What does the writer seem to think of the characters described in the story?

   _____

   _____

   _____

3. What major events are described in the story?

   _____

   _____

   _____

4. What do you think is the theme or message of the story?

   _____

   _____

   _____

Tips for Reading a Nonfiction Passage

As you read a piece of nonfiction, ask yourself the following questions:

- What is the title?

- Who is the author?

- What is the subject of the piece?

- What is the author's thesis, or main idea?

- What is the primary purpose of the piece? To tell a story? To describe? To persuade? To inform?

- How is the information organized? What information might be most important?

Be sure to note important people, places, facts, dates, events, causes, effects, similarities, differences, steps in a process, and questions or opinions presented by the writer.

Chapter 6

A Tale to Tell

Understanding Fiction

What Is Fiction?

Fiction is writing about made-up people, places, and events. Most of the fiction that you will read in school and on reading tests is in the form of narratives, or stories. The story "The Fox and the Crow" on page 95 is an example of fiction. It is a story about imaginary characters and events.

Here are some things you should look for as you read a story or piece of fiction:

Features of Fiction

Characters	The **characters** are the people, animals, or other creatures who take part in the story.
Setting	The **setting** is where and when the story takes place. Longer stories and books often have more than one setting.
Conflict	The **conflict** is the problem or struggle that the main character faces.
Theme	The **theme** is the main idea or lesson of the story.

You may have noticed that the features of a fictional story are very similar to those of a nonfiction narrative. There are characters. There is a setting. There is a theme, or message, that the writer wants to get across. The characters may face a series of problems as the **plot,** or sequence of events, unfolds. In most fictional narratives, however, there is one main problem that the main character must overcome. The main problem is the **conflict.** By looking at the way the main character deals with the conflict, we learn the theme, or message, of the story.

Analyzing Fiction

"The Fox and the Crow" is a **fable** by Æsop. As in other fables, the **characters** are animals—a fox and a crow—and the story is told to make a point. The main character is the fox. The **setting** is morningtime in the woods. The **main conflict** is that Fox is hungry and wants the piece of meat that Crow is holding in her beak. Fox keeps trying to trick Crow by complimenting her and asking her questions. He hopes that she will open her beak to answer and drop the meat. At first, she does not fall for his trickery, but then Fox praises her singing and asks for a song. At last, Crow cannot resist. When she opens her beak to sing, she drops the meat and Fox runs off with it.

Based on this information, you can make a good guess about what message the writer is trying to get across. The **theme** of this story is *Watch out for false praise.*

As you read a story, you should ask yourself the following questions:

Questions to Ask When Reading Fiction

1. Who are the characters?

2. Where is the story set?

3. What is the main conflict, or problem?

4. How does the main character deal with the conflict?

5. What theme, or message, is the author trying to get across?

Exercise *Read the story below. As you read, ask yourself the questions in the chart on the previous page. Then answer the questions that follow the story. Be sure to write in complete sentences.*

The Shoemaker and the Elves

Once there was a poor shoemaker who barely had enough money to feed himself and his family. One night, he found he had only enough leather for one pair of shoes. He cut the pieces for the shoes and left them on the table to be stitched together the next morning. When he woke up, he shouted in happy surprise. He found the shoes already made. They were so beautiful that a customer gave him more than the usual price for them.

With this money, the shoemaker bought enough leather to make two pairs of shoes. Again, he cut the pieces out and went to bed. When he awoke, he found on his table two beautifully made pairs of shoes. They, too, were quickly sold. Every day the shoemaker sold as many shoes as he had cut out. From then on, the shoemaker began to grow rich. Every night he cut out pieces, and every morning he found them beautifully put together.

One night he said to his wife, "Let us hide and see who our helpers are." At bedtime, the shoemaker and his wife hid themselves in the corner. Before long, two tiny elves appeared. They were dressed in rags, but they merrily went right to work. They quickly sewed up the shoes and disappeared. The wife said, "The poor little dears have made us

rich, but they are dressed in rags. Let's show them our thanks." She made each elf a colorful little suit of clothes, and the shoemaker made them tiny boots.

The next night, the shoemaker and his wife hid themselves in the corner again. They watched to see how their gifts would be received. When the elves appeared, they found the clothes and put them on. They danced happily about and sang:

"Fine folks in fine clothes are we!
No more shoemakers will we be."

And they kept their word. Never again did the elf helpers come to sew his shoes, but the shoemaker and his wife lived in peace and plenty ever after. o

1. Who is the main character in the story, and what conflict, or problem, does this character face? How is the character's problem solved?

_____

_____

_____

_____

_____

2. What message is the writer trying to get across by telling this story? Do you think the shoemaker and his wife wished they had not given the elves their gift?

_____

_____

_____

_____

_____

_____

Chapter 7

Words That Sing

Understanding Poetry

What Is Poetry?

Do you ever sing along to your favorite song? Just about everybody does. Songs are easy to remember. They have rhythm. They usually have words that rhyme. If you write down the words of a song, you can say them instead of singing them. You may notice that, even without the music, the words have a rhythm. The lyrics of songs are one kind of **poetry.**

Poets use words in special ways to help get across their feelings, thoughts, and ideas. Poets use many techniques to make their language sound musical and therefore interesting or appealing. This chapter will talk about some of the special ways that poets use words, so that you will know what to look for and pay attention to when you read poetry.

The Sounds of Poetry

Poets often use the sounds of words in special ways. Many poems have rhythm and rhyme. Sometimes several words in a poem begin or end with the same sound. At other times, words in a poem sound like what they mean. An example of this kind of word is *chirp.* This section describes some of the many sounds of poetry.

Rhythm

Songs have beats. Poems also have beats. Each word part, or syllable, has a beat. The beat can be strong, or it can be weak. For example, the word *party* has two syllables: *par–* and *–ty.* Say the word out loud. Notice that you say *par–* a little louder and stronger than *–ty.* In this word, *par–* is the strong beat, and *–ty* is the weak beat. **Rhythm** is the pattern of strong and weak beats in a poem.

Read this poem. Pay attention to the beats.

The Land of Counterpane
Robert Louis Stevenson

When I was sick and lay a-bed
I had two pillows at my head,
And all my toys beside me lay
To keep me happy all the day.

"The Land of Counterpane" has a regular pattern of strong and weak beats. The first line begins with a weak beat. It is followed by a strong beat. The rest of the line follows the same pattern. Strong beats in poetry are marked with a ʹ.

Weak beats are marked with a ˘, as shown here:

˘ ´ ˘ ´ ˘ ´ ˘ ´
When I was sick and lay a-bed

Now read the last line. Try to figure out the pattern of beats.

To keep me happy all the day.

This line also begins with a weak beat. Did you figure out the pattern?

Rhyme

Say these words: *mice, rice, nice.* How are these words alike? You probably know that they rhyme. **Rhyme** is the repetition of sounds at the ends of words. *Mice, rice,* and *nice* rhyme because they all end with *ice.*

Read this poem. Watch for the words that rhyme.

Just Me
Margaret Hillert

Nobody sees what I can **see,**
Far back of my eyes there is only **me.**
And nobody knows how my thoughts
 begin,
For there's only myself inside my skin.

Look at the words *see* and *me* at the end of the first two lines. They rhyme. Now look at the words *begin* and *skin* at the end of the next two lines. They rhyme, too. Write an *a* next to the boldfaced words *see* and *me.* Write a *b* next to the underlined words *begin* and *skin.* Now you can see that the **rhyme scheme,** or pattern of rhyme, in this poem is *aabb.*

This poem has a different rhyme scheme:

My Mother's Hands
Anna Hempstead Branch

My mother's hands are cool and fair,
 They can do anything.
Delicate mercies hide them there,
 Like flowers in the spring.

Can you name this rhyme scheme? If you said *abab,* you are right. The words *fair* and *there* rhyme. The letter *a* stands for these words. The words *anything* and *spring* rhyme. The letter *b* stands for these words.

Assonance

In addition to rhyme, poets use a technique called assonance. Words that rhyme often have the same vowel sound and the same final consonant sound, as in *mice, rice,* and *nice.* **Assonance** is when a writer uses words that have the same vowel sound in the stressed syllable but that end with *different* consonant sounds. Let's look at an example from the poem "Just Me" on this page. In the line "And nobody knows how my thoughts begin," the words *nobody* and *knows* have the same vowel sound (long *o*), but they end with different consonant sounds. In the last line, the words *inside* and *skin* both have the short *i* sound.

Your Turn

Exercise A *Read each poem. Look for the words that rhyme. Fill in the circle next to the correct rhyme scheme.*

1. In the Summer When I Go to Bed
Thomas Hood

I'd like to be a tall giraffe
Making lots of people laugh,
I'd do a tap dance in the street
With little bells upon my feet.

Ⓐ *abba*
Ⓑ *baab*
Ⓒ *abab*
Ⓓ *aabb*

2. Peas
Anonymous

I eat my peas with honey,
I've done it all my life.
It makes the peas taste funny,
But it keeps them on my knife.

Ⓐ *aabb*
Ⓑ *abba*
Ⓒ *abab*
Ⓓ *baab*

3. Blossoms
Frank Dempster Sherman

Out of my window I could see
But yesterday, upon the tree,
The blossoms white, like tufts of snow
That had forgotten when to go.

Ⓐ *abab*
Ⓑ *aabb*
Ⓒ *baab*
Ⓓ *abba*

Exercise B *The following lines come from the poems in Exercise A. Mark the strong and weak beats in each line using these marks: ′ and ˘.*

1. I'd like to be a tall giraffe

2. It makes the peas taste funny,

3. That had forgotten when to go.

Exercise C *Read the poem and underline words that have the same vowel sound but end with different consonant sounds.*

No one ate the sponge cake.

They liked the icing best.

They licked it off till it was gone,

And only bare cake was left.

Understanding Poetry

Alliteration

Alliteration is another technique of sound that poets use. **Alliteration** is the repetition of the same sound at the beginnings of words. These sounds draw attention to something about the poem. The sounds might emphasize the poem's title. They might also emphasize the topic, idea, message, or feeling that the writer wants to get across.

Read this poem. Look for the *s* sound at the beginnings of words.

Fly Away, Swallow
Christina Rossetti

Fly away, fly away, over the sea,
Sun-loving swallow, for summer
is done.
Come again, come again, come
back to me,
Bringing the summer and
bringing the sun.

The words *sea, sun, swallow,* and *summer* begin with *s*. The use of these *s* words together is an example of alliteration. The soft *s* sound emphasizes things about summer, such as sun, sea, and swallows. Notice that the third line does not have any *s* words. The sound repeated in this line is the hard *c,* like the cold of winter. The final line emphasizes the speaker's strong feelings. It expresses her hope that summer will come again soon.

Onomatopoeia

Another sound technique that poets use is onomatopoeia. **Onomatopoeia** is the use of words that sound like what they mean. Some examples are *buzz, honk, beep,* and *meow.*

Read "Froggie, Froggie." Find an example of a word that sounds like what it means.

Froggie, Froggie
Anonymous

Froggie, froggie.
Hoppity-hop!
When you get to the lake
You do not stop.
Plop!

The word *plop* sounds like what it means. *Plop* is an example of onomatopoeia.

Exercise A *Read these lines of poetry. Underline the words that are examples of onomatopoeia.*

1. **Sunning**
   James S. Tippett

   Old Dog lay in the summer sun

   Much too lazy to rise and run.

   He flapped an ear

   At a buzzing fly;

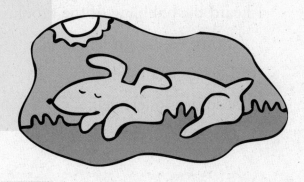

2. **The New England Boy's Song about Thanksgiving Day**
   Lydia Maria Child

   Over the river, and through the wood,

      To have a first-rate play—

         Hear the bells ring

         Ting a ling ding,

   Hurrah for Thanksgiving day!

3. **The Storm**
   Sara Coleridge

   The heavens are scowling,

   The thunder is growling,

   The loud winds are howling,

      The storm has come suddenly on!

More ▶

Exercise B *Remember that alliteration is the repetition of sounds at the beginnings of words. Underline the examples of alliteration in each poem below.*

1. **August**
   Katharine Pyle

   I heard the bubbling of the brook;

      At times an acorn fell,

   And far away a robin sang

      Deep in a lonely dell.

2. **The Flea and the Fly**
   Anonymous

   A flea and a fly got caught in a flue.

      Said the fly, "Let us flee."

      Said the flea, "Let us fly."

   So together they flew through a flaw in the flue.

3. **Have You Ever Seen?**
   Anonymous

   Have you ever seen a sheet on a river bed?

   Or a single hair from a hammer's head?

   Has the foot of a mountain any toes?

   And is there a pair of garden hose?

Understanding Poetry

Meaning in Poetry

Most poems have a message. The poet wants you to learn something from the poem. The message of a poem is its **theme.** It is the main idea.

Read the poem "The Little Elf," below. As you read, think about the message the poet is trying to get across.

The Little Elf
by John Kendrick Bangs

I met a little Elf-man, once,

    Down where the lilies blow.[1]

I asked him why he was so small,

    And why he did not grow.

He slightly frowned, and with his eye

    He looked me through and through

"I'm quite as big for me," said he,

    "As you are big for you."

The speaker in the poem is the person who met the little elf. We know that elves don't really exist. So, we know that the speaker either imagined that he met a little elf, or he is pretending that he met one, just to make a point. The speaker asks the elf why he is so small and why he doesn't grow. We can tell that the elf is offended, because he frowns. The elf points out that he is the size that he should be, just as the speaker is the size that he should be. The theme, or message, might be that everyone is different, and that those differences are normal.

When you are trying to figure out the theme of a poem, it is helpful to restate each line of the poem in your own words. Then you can make sure that you understand what is going on in the poem.

---

[1]**blow.** Blossom. This is an archaic, or old-fashioned, usage.

Exercise Read this poem. Think about the theme. Remember that the theme is the main idea, or message, of the poem. Then fill in the circle next to the sentence that best describes the poem's theme.

Our House
Dorothy Brown Thompson

Our house is small—
    The lawn and all
Can scarcely hold the flower,
        Yet every bit,
        The whole of it,
Is precious, for it's ours.
        From door to door,
        From roof to floor,
From wall to wall we love it;
        We wouldn't change
        For something strange
One shabby corner of it!

Ⓐ The lawn for this house has no flowers.

Ⓑ A person's house is special because it belongs to him or her.

Ⓒ The house in the poem is a shabby one.

Ⓓ New houses make better homes than old houses.

Return to the exercises at the beginning of the unit. Check your work and fix it if necessary. Give the exercises to your teacher for grading.

Unit 4

Listening, Notetaking, and Graphic Organizers

DO NOT read the following story. Your teacher will read it aloud to you. As you listen to this true tale of the life of a great African American leader, take notes about information that you think might be important to remember. Then use your notes to answer the questions that follow the story.

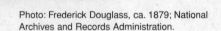

Photo: Frederick Douglass, ca. 1879; National Archives and Records Administration.

From Slave to Civil Rights Leader

by Almira Tweed

In his six years, Frederick had seen his mother only a few times. She was a slave on a big farm. He lived nearby with his grandmother, who took care of him while his mother worked.

One day, Frederick's grandmother took him on a long walk to another farm. There he began his life as a slave. He had to work long hours with no comforts. He was always hungry. Frederick and the other slave children ate cornmeal from a long dish called a trough. Farm animals are fed in troughs. The children used seashells to scoop out the food.

Frederick was often cold. He wore only a torn shirt that came down to his knees. He saw many slaves being beaten. He was beaten himself. Worst of all, he saw families torn apart. Children were sold away from their parents. Once family members were separated, they rarely saw one another again. Frederick's own mother died when he was about seven. No one told him she was sick. No one took him to see her before she died.

When Frederick turned eight, he was sent to the city. His master's wife, Sophia, started to teach him to read. When the master found out, he was very angry. The master did not want slaves to read. He thought that if slaves learned to read, they would be able to think for themselves. The master did not want that.

Even though Sophia stopped teaching him, Frederick did not stop learning. He made friends with white boys and asked them questions about what they were learning in school. He found books and studied them in secret. He bought a book of speeches about liberty. **Liberty** means a person's right to be free and live in the way he or she thinks best. Frederick practiced saying the speeches out loud. He wanted to become free. He also wanted to help others become free.

While he was still young, Frederick started a secret school. He taught other slaves to read, write, and think for

Painting: Douglass edited the first Negro paper "The North Star"; Jacob Lawrence, painter (b.1917); National Archives and Records Administration.

themselves. When he was twenty, he risked his life to escape to the North. There he gave speeches about liberty. He became a leader in the fight against slavery.

Frederick wrote a book about his life. The book was called *Narrative of the Life of Frederick Douglass*. A **narrative** is a story. Frederick's book opened many people's eyes to what slavery was really like. Because of his hard work and the work of many others, slavery in the United States finally ended. Frederick Douglass is still known as one of the greatest leaders in the struggle for liberty. ○

Listening, Notetaking, and Graphic Organizers (149)

Your Turn

Exercise A *Fill in the circle next to the correct answer to each question.*

1. What is the main idea of the article?
   - Ⓐ Slaves suffered horrible conditions and were often treated cruelly by their masters.
   - Ⓑ Slave children were forced to eat out of troughs, like animals.
   - Ⓒ Frederick Douglass rose from slavery to become one of the greatest leaders in the struggle for liberty.
   - Ⓓ Frederick Douglass taught other slaves to read.

2. Which of the following events happened FIRST?
   - Ⓐ Frederick was sent to the city.
   - Ⓑ Frederick's mother passed away.
   - Ⓒ Frederick learned to read.
   - Ⓓ Frederick escaped to the North.

3. Why did Sophia (Frederick's master's wife) stop teaching Frederick how to read?
   - Ⓐ Frederick was a slow learner, so Sophia grew impatient with him.
   - Ⓑ Frederick was sent away to work in the fields.
   - Ⓒ Sophia became sick and was not able to teach him any more.
   - Ⓓ Frederick's master demanded that Sophia stop teaching Frederick.

4. Which of the following is NOT one of the achievements of Frederick Douglass mentioned in the story?
   - Ⓐ He helped other slaves escape to the North.
   - Ⓑ He started a secret school and taught other slaves to read and write.
   - Ⓒ He wrote a book about his life.
   - Ⓓ He gave speeches about liberty.

5. Which of the following words BEST describes Frederick Douglass?
   - Ⓐ shy
   - Ⓑ courageous
   - Ⓒ disrespectful
   - Ⓓ depressed

Exercise B *Frederick was a special person. He was smart and brave, and he cared about other people. Write about what made Frederick Douglass special.*

In your writing, describe

- something from the story that shows Frederick was smart.
- something that shows he was brave.
- something that shows that he cared about other people.

Use the lines below to make a rough outline of your piece of writing. Write your first draft on a separate piece of paper. Revise your draft using the checklist on page 196. Then make a clean final copy.

_____

_____

_____

_____

_____

_____

_____

_____

_____

_____

_____

_____

_____

Chapter 8

Hold That Thought

Introduction to Notetaking

It is important to know how to take good notes. Knowing how to take good notes will help you on the ELA exam. It will also help you in all your other schoolwork.

What Are Notes?

Imagine that you are at home and the telephone rings. Someone from your dentist's office is calling to remind you that you have an appointment next Tuesday afternoon at 4:30. You could simply try to remember when you need to go there. A better idea, however, is to write the day and time on a piece of paper.

Writing down short reminders and important facts when you read or listen is called **taking notes.** Notes are useful because they help you to remember important things.

When to Take Notes

Take notes whenever you are listening to or reading something important that you might need to remember later. You should take notes in a notebook when listening to your teacher in class. You should also take notes when you are reading for homework. It is **very important** for you to take notes during the ELA exam.

Notetaking Tips

1. Take notes on important information that you need to remember.

2. Take notes when you listen to your teacher in school.

3. Take notes when you read for school.

4. Take notes when you read or listen to a passage during the ELA exam or any other exam.

5. Take notes to organize your ideas before you begin to write about a topic.

How to Take Notes

When you take notes, do not try to write down every word. Writing down everything that you hear or read is impossible. Instead, write down only the most important information. Do not use complete sentences in your notes. Instead, use words and parts of sentences. Read the following story about a famous explorer:

Henry Hudson was a daring explorer who set sail from England in the early 1600s in search of a northern passage to Asia. Such a passage would have made trade with China much easier and cheaper for Europeans, and many explorers went in search of it, hoping for great wealth. Hudson sailed to the east, north of Russia, and to the west, north of North America, but icy waters kept forcing him to turn back. Finally, the English company that had paid for his voyages gave up and refused to fund any more of his explorations. But the Dutch East India Company was not so easily discouraged. They gave Hudson a ship and supplies for another voyage. This time, he sailed farther south, hoping to find a passage through the North American continent. He stumbled upon the Hudson River (which was later named after him) and sailed as far as Albany before turning back. Later on, the Dutch claimed the area that Hudson had explored and named it New Amsterdam. Eventually, it came to be called New York. ○

Henry Hudson's Half Moon, 1609, anchored in Hudson River, NY.

Introduction to Notetaking

Notes on this paragraph might look like this:

> Henry Hudson = daring explorer
> —Set sail from England in early 1600s
> —Was looking for no. passage to Asia = better trade w/ China
> —Went north of Russia and N.A. → waters too icy
> —Eng. company gave up but Dutch East India Co. funded another voyage
> —Sailed farther south & stumbled upon Hudson R. (named after him)
> —Dutch later claimed area & called it New Amsterdam → now NY

Notice that the student did not use complete sentences in these notes. Instead, the notes are in **phrases,** short groups of words. Also notice that the main idea is written at the left-hand margin. Important details about each main idea are written below it. Each detail is listed after a dash (—). Look back at the paragraph on whales on page 88. Here is an example of notes about that paragraph:

> Whales
> —Over 75 kinds
> —2 groups: toothed & baleen
> Toothed whales
> —Hunt fish, squid
> —Sperm Whale = largest toothed whale
> Baleen whales
> —No teeth
> —Long strips called baleen strain food
> —Scoop up/gulp food
> —Eat shrimp, tiny fish
> —Blue Whale = baleen whale (largest animal on Earth)

More Notetaking Tips

1. Do not try to take down every word.

2. Use single words or phrases, not complete sentences.

3. Write the subject at the top. Write the main ideas on separate lines, starting at the left-hand margin. Write details about each main idea underneath it, starting with a dash (—).

4. Use symbols and abbreviations when taking notes.

Using Symbols and Abbreviations in Notes

When you take notes, you have to write fast, especially if you are taking notes on something that someone is saying or reading out loud. One way to get information down fast is to use symbols and abbreviations. A **symbol** is a sign, like + for the word *and*. An **abbreviation** is a short form of a word. The following chart lists some symbols and abbreviations to use when taking notes:

Symbols and Abbreviations for Notetaking

Symbol	Meaning	Abbreviation	Meaning
+ *or* &	and	w/	with
–	not *or* minus	w/o	without
*	important	ex.	example
=	equals *or* is	1st	first
Δ	change	2nd	second
→	therefore *or* causes	3rd	third
		4th	fourth

Abbreviation	Meaning
Amer.	American
U.S.	United States
N.Y.	New York

Feel free to make up your own symbols and abbreviations. Be sure that you will be able to understand what you wrote when you look back at your notes later.

Your Turn

Exercise A *Your teacher will read this passage aloud to you. Take notes as you listen to the passage. Some notes have been started for you on the next page. Use that page to take your notes.*

How do animals "talk" to each other? We know that they do not use words. Instead, animals use sounds, body movements and expressions, and even smell to send messages.

Many animals communicate through sound. Dogs howl, whine, snarl, and bark. Dolphins "talk" in squeaks and whistles. Male humpback whales sing complex songs. Each song has a distinct theme and melody. The songs can last up to twenty minutes. They can be heard by other humpback whales across the ocean. Scientists are not sure why whales sing. Some think the songs are used to attract mates. Others believe the songs may be a warning to other males to stay away.

Other animals communicate through movement and facial expressions. In addition to communicating through sound, dogs use body movements. When two dogs meet, the weaker one may lie down to show that it is not a threat. Bees "talk" by doing a special dance. A bee will dance in a figure-eight to tell other bees where food is. White storks nest in high places, such as in trees and on rooftops or chimneys. Both the male and female stork take turns sitting on their eggs. A white stork who has been gone for a while will swing its head over its back and clap its beak. This is how a stork greets its mate when he or she comes back to the nest. Expressions are another kind of movement used by animals to show their feelings. Bared teeth and glaring eyes show that an animal is ready to attack. Apes can show anger, fear, and happiness with their faces.

Many animals use smell to send messages. Dogs, foxes, wolves, and even rhinos mark their territory by leaving their scent. Scents also contain information about the animal, such as its age and its gender (male or female). ○

Finish these notes by filling in the blanks below.

Animal Language

—Animals use sound, body movements & expressions, & _____

Sound

—Dogs _____

—Dolphins squeak & _____

—Humpback whales _____

Movement & facial expressions

—Dogs _____

—Bees _____

—White storks _____

—Apes _____

Smell

—Dogs, foxes, wolves, & rhinos mark territory

—Information from scents = age & gender (M/F)

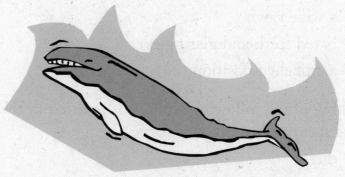

More ▶

Your Turn

Exercise B *Now use your notes on the passage to answer the questions below. Fill in the circle next to the correct answer to each question.*

1. Which of the following does the passage say a dog might do when it meets a more powerful dog?
   - Ⓐ bare its teeth and growl
   - Ⓑ circle the other dog
   - Ⓒ lie down
   - Ⓓ whimper

2. How does a bee "tell" other bees where food is?
   - Ⓐ It brings a bit of the food back to the hive.
   - Ⓑ It dances in a figure-eight.
   - Ⓒ It buzzes loudly.
   - Ⓓ It stings a person or animal near the food.

3. Why does a white stork swing its head over its back and clap its beak?
   - Ⓐ to let its mate know that it has returned to the nest
   - Ⓑ to show how much it likes to sit on the nest
   - Ⓒ to throw food into the nest
   - Ⓓ to scare away predators

4. According to the passage, which of the following "expressions" shows that an animal is ready to attack?
   - Ⓐ a tail held between the legs
   - Ⓑ a wide yawn
   - Ⓒ bared teeth and glaring eyes
   - Ⓓ a crouched position

5. Which of the following animals isn't listed in the passage as one that uses scent to mark its territory?
   - Ⓐ dog
   - Ⓑ whale
   - Ⓒ wolf
   - Ⓓ rhino

Chapter 9

Picture This!

Taking Notes with Graphic Organizers

In the previous chapter, you learned how to take notes in the form of a rough outline. In this chapter, you will learn how to use a chart or picture when you take notes. A **graphic organizer** is a chart or picture that you use for notetaking.

Using Word Webs

One way to take notes is to use a **word web.** It is simple to make a word web. First, write down the main subject and put a circle around it. Then write details in circles grouped around the subject. Draw lines to connect details to the subject, as shown below. Read the paragraph about Blackbeard first. Then look at this example of the word-web notes for the paragraph about him.

Blackbeard

The most frightening pirate in early America was an Englishman named Edward Teach. Teach was known as "Blackbeard." Blackbeard had a thick, black beard and long, black hair that he wore in braids or dreadlocks. When he was about to attack a ship, he braided fuse cords (from cannons) into his hair and beard. The smoking fuses under his hat made it lmook as if smoke were coming out of his head. Blackbeard was very dangerous, even for a pirate. His raids on ships soon spread fear up and down the coast. His pirate flag, the Jolly Roger, showed a picture of a skeleton. The captain of any ship that got close enough to spot Blackbeard's Jolly Roger knew he was in big trouble.

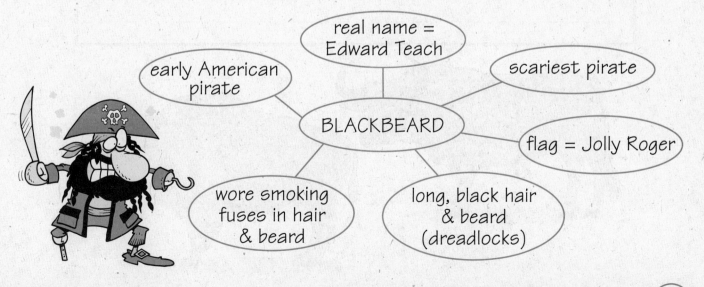

Using Charts

Yet another way to take notes is to make a **chart.** Charts are good for taking notes that compare two subjects. Here is a paragraph that compares two animals—the buffalo and the bison. Look at the notes (in chart form) below this paragraph.

Buffalo & Bison

Two animals that people often confuse are the buffalo and the bison. The water buffalo lives in Asia; the Cape buffalo lives in Africa. The American bison lives in North America. The European bison, or wisent, lives in eastern Europe and Russia, where it is very rare. A bison has a large hump on its back, shaggy hair, and short horns. A buffalo has long, curving horns and short hair. The water buffalo is often used as a farm animal in Asia. It pulls plows in the rice fields. Bison have never been tamed to do work on farms. Bison were once hunted until they almost disappeared. Today, most bison live in herds that roam protected areas in the wild, like national parks.

Buffalo & Bison	
Buffalo	**Bison**
Lives in Asia & Africa	Lives in N. America & Europe
Has short hair & long horns	Has shaggy hair & short horns
Is used as a farm animal	Lives in the wild in protected areas

Other Graphic Organizers

Two other widely used graphic organizers are timelines and Venn diagrams.

Timeline (Use to show times and events)

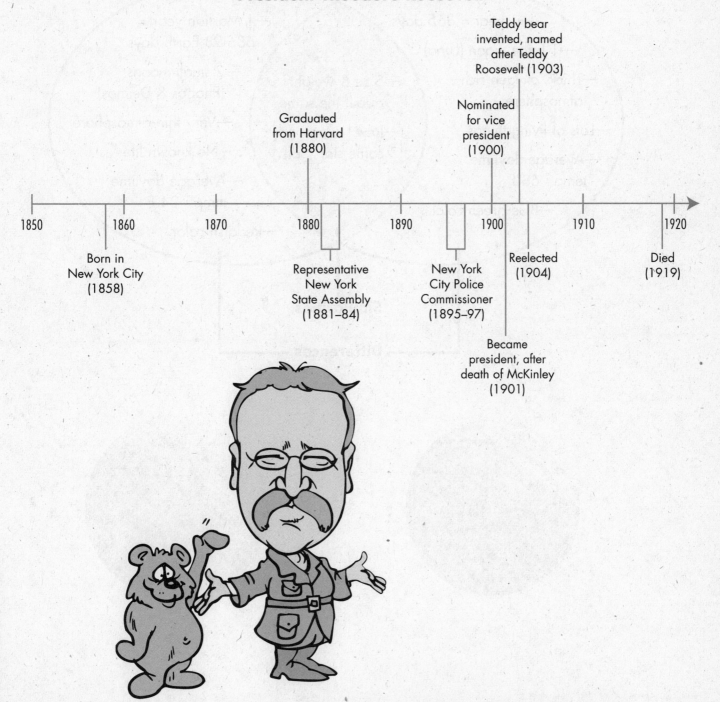

President Theodore Roosevelt

Teddy bear invented, named after Teddy Roosevelt (1903)

Nominated for vice president (1900)

Graduated from Harvard (1880)

1850   1860   1870   1880   1890   1900   1910   1920

Born in New York City (1858)

Representative New York State Assembly (1881–84)

New York City Police Commissioner (1895–97)

Reelected (1904)

Died (1919)

Became president, after death of McKinley (1901)

Venn Diagram (Use to compare and contrast)

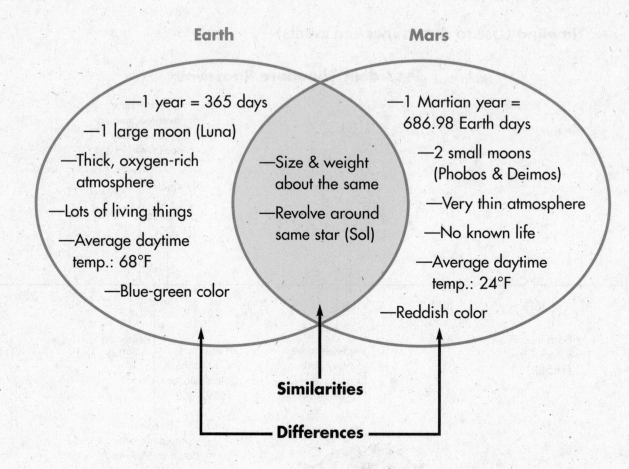

Earth

Mars

—1 year = 365 days

—1 large moon (Luna)

—Thick, oxygen-rich atmosphere

—Lots of living things

—Average daytime temp.: 68°F

—Blue-green color

—Size & weight about the same

—Revolve around same star (Sol)

—1 Martian year = 686.98 Earth days

—2 small moons (Phobos & Deimos)

—Very thin atmosphere

—No known life

—Average daytime temp.: 24°F

—Reddish color

Similarities

Differences

Your Turn

Exercise A *Use a word web to take notes on this short passage about energy sources. The notes have been started for you.*

Energy is the power that we use to run the machines and lights and other modern conveniences that we use each day. At the present time, there are three main types of energy source: fossil fuels, nuclear, and renewable. Fossil fuels are burned to release energy. Examples of fossil fuels include coal, oil, and natural gas. Fossil fuels are widely used, but they cause pollution and global warming. Nuclear energy is released by breaking apart or putting together atoms. Nuclear power plants can produce a lot of power cheaply. However, they make wastes that are dangerous and difficult to dispose of safely. Renewable energy sources include solar power (power from the sun), wind power, and wave power. These forms of energy are not as reliable as the others. For the time being, they are fairly expensive to produce, but they are very, very safe and do not cause pollution. And, as the word "renewable" shows, they are not likely to run out.

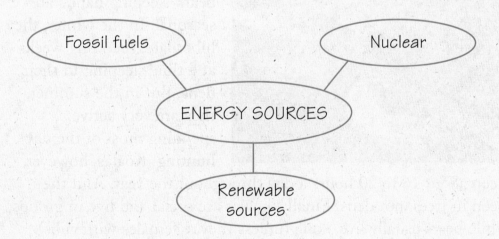

More ▶

Exercise B *Use a chart to take notes on this short passage about koalas and bears. Takes notes on your own paper.*

If you have ever seen a picture of a koala (or seen a real one!) then it is easy to understand why these creatures are often referred to as "koala bears." Like bears, they have a thick fur coat, and they climb trees. In fact, they look a lot like teddy bears. However, koalas are not bears. Both animals are mammals, but only the koala is a marsupial. That means that baby koalas are born before they are fully developed. Then they crawl into their mother's pouch, where they live until they are big enough to survive in the outside world.

Bears, like most mammals, give birth to fully developed young. Another difference between koalas and bears is their diet. Koalas eat only plants, particularly the leaves of eucalyptus trees. Bears, on the other hand, eat plants and meat. While both creatures sleep a lot, bears' sleeping habits are seasonal. In the winter, they hibernate, spending weeks at a time sleeping in their dens. But in the summer, they are very active, spending most of the day hunting. Koalas, however, sleep about 16 to 20 hours a day throughout the year. And they sleep in trees, not dens. Finally, koalas are social and live in groups, while bears usually live alone (unless they're females with cubs). So next time you say, "What a cute koala," leave off the "bear" to help avoid the confusion. ◦

Exercise C *Read the short story below. Then, on your own paper, take notes in a chart that compares and contrasts the two girls and their families.*

Nola and Tina
by Sally Hines

Nola and Tina were friends. They were friends in school, and they were friends after school. If the girls went to Nola's home after school, they took the bus uptown. Nola lived fifty blocks away from the school. Tina liked to go to Nola's apartment. There was so much room. Nola had her own room. Nola's grandmother had a bedroom and a studio. The apartment where Nola's family lived had eight rooms in all.

At Nola's home, they ate cheese and crackers. Sometimes they colored. Nola was good at coloring. Sometimes they played cards with Nola's grandmother. Nola called her grandmother by her first name, Susan.

Nola also loved to go to Tina's apartment. When Nola went home with Tina after school, they walked. Tina lived only one block from the school. Nola liked going to Tina's apartment because everyone there was so friendly. There were lots of kids. Tina had three sisters and a baby brother. She called her mother Mommy and her father Poppie. She called her grandmother Mama Lou. Somehow seven people fit into five rooms, and there was always room for friends. At Tina's, the girls made English muffin pizzas for a snack. Then they pretended to be actors and made up plays. Tina was a great actor. She liked to make up sad plays about grownup ladies with big problems. She could make herself and Nola cry. Afterwards, they played with baby Jimmy.

Whether they were at Tina's house or Nola's house, the friends had fun. ○

Chapter 10

Listen Up!

Listening and Taking Notes

In the last two chapters, you learned how to take notes. Now you know how to take notes using rough outlines and graphic organizers. In this chapter, you will learn about what to write down when you are taking notes as you listen. What you take down in your notes will depend upon the type of piece you are reading.

Active Listening

Have you ever heard someone say, "I just want to veg out in front of the television"? What does it mean to "veg out"? It means "to look and listen without thinking much or doing much of anything." This is exactly what you *should not* do when you listen for a test or in class.

When you listen in class or for a test, do not "veg out." Instead, try to listen actively. That is, think about what you are hearing. Use the same strategies that you use for active reading:

- Ask **questions** about what you are hearing.
- **Visualize** what you are hearing. That is, create pictures of it in your mind.
- Make **predictions,** or guesses, about what will happen next.
- After a while, **summarize,** or put into fewer words, what you have heard so far.
- **Connect** what you are hearing to your own life and to what you already know.

Listen for **main ideas**—the most important ideas—and for the details that support the main ideas. As you listen, take careful notes. Use a rough outline and/or graphic organizers.

For the listening part of the ELA test, you will listen to a selection twice. The first time that you hear it, think carefully as you listen. Use the active listening strategies listed above. The second time that you hear it, take notes as you listen.

Listening and Taking Notes on Stories

When you listen to a passage, decide whether it is a story (narrative) or some other kind of piece. A **story** tells about something that happens or a series of events that happen. The events are called the **plot.** A story can be true (**nonfiction**) or imaginary (**fiction**).

The chart below shows some of what you should take notes on when the passage is **fiction**—a story about imaginary characters, places, and events:

Important Notes for Stories about Characters

- The **title** of the story
- The **author** of the story (the person who wrote it)
- The **setting** (time and place of the story)
- The main **characters** (people or animals in the story)
- Details that tell what the characters are like
- Reasons why characters act the way they do
- Problems or conflicts that the characters face
- Important **events,** or happenings
- The **theme** (any lesson taught by the story)

Listening and Taking Notes on Nonfiction

As you know, **nonfiction** is writing about real people, places, and events. The next chart shows what kind of notes you should take when the passage you are listening to is nonfiction.

Important Notes for Selections That Give Facts

- The **title** and **author**
- The **subject** (what the story is mostly about)
- The names of **people** and **places** mentioned in the story
- The **main ideas** (the most important ideas in each part of the story)
- **Supporting details** (details that support the main ideas)

Practice taking notes as you listen by doing the exercises on the following pages. Also, take notes as you listen in class and on all the reading that you do for school.

Your Turn

Exercise A Your teacher will read aloud to you the story below. As you listen, take notes on the story. Then use your notes to answer the questions that follow the story. Be sure to write in complete sentences.

The Man, the Boy, and the Donkey
A folktale

A man was going to market to sell his donkey, and his son begged to come along. The two set off toward town, walking beside the donkey.

By and by, they passed some young girls, who giggled and pointed at them. "How silly to walk instead of riding the donkey! After all, what is a donkey for?" the girls asked.

Papa heard them and told his son to climb on the donkey. Then no one would laugh at them.

Soon they passed two old men on the road. "Look at that lazy boy riding the donkey while his father has to walk," they sneered.

So Papa said, "Son, come down and let me ride the donkey."

More ▶

As they came into town, they were met by some women. "Did you ever see so lazy a fellow?" they cried. "He rides the donkey while that poor little boy can hardly keep up!"

"What shall we do?" said Papa. "How can we please everyone?" He thought and thought. Finally, he came up with a plan. "My son, climb on the donkey with me. Then everyone will be happy."

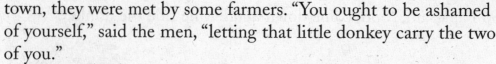

So the man and his son rode on the donkey together. In the town, they were met by some farmers. "You ought to be ashamed of yourself," said the men, "letting that little donkey carry the two of you."

"You are right," said the man. "It is too heavy a load for him."

The man did not know what to do. "We do not want people in the town to see us both riding the donkey," he told his son. He thought and thought and suddenly said, "I have it! We will carry the donkey!"

They grunted and groaned and gasped and wheezed. They finally got the donkey onto their shoulders. As they traveled toward the market, all the people laughed at the strange sight.

When the man and his son tried to sell the donkey, everyone said, "Who wants to buy a donkey that has to be carried?"

So, the man and his son returned home without selling the donkey. "I think we have learned a lesson, my son," said Papa. "If you try to please everyone, you please no one." ○

1. Who are the characters in the story? Who is the main character, and what conflict, or problem, does this character face? How does the character try to solve this problem?

_____

_____

_____

_____

_____

_____

2. What message is the writer trying to get across by telling this story? Do you think this is an important message? Why?

_____

_____

_____

_____

_____

_____

More ▶

Your Turn

Exercise B *Your teacher will read aloud to you this passage about clouds. As you listen, take notes on your own paper. Then use your notes to answer the questions that follow.*

Can You Sit on a Cloud?
by Virginia Leigh

It is fun to look up at the sky and watch the clouds. The clouds seem to make shapes in the sky. They can look like people, like animals, or like objects made out of fluffy white cotton. If you watch a cloud long enough, its shape changes. That is because the wind is blowing on it. Although it looks as if you could sit on a cloud, clouds are not really solid. They are loose collections of small droplets of water. The water in the air collects around bits of dust or smoke and forms clouds.

There are a few different kinds of clouds. Clouds come in different shapes. They also form at different heights above the Earth. The three main kinds of clouds are cumulus, stratus, and cirrus.

Cumulus means "heap." Cumulus clouds are the ones that look like big soft heaps of cotton. You usually see cumulus clouds when the weather is fair. If these clouds become very thick and dark and rise in high banks, they can become storm clouds. *Thunderheads* are a kind of cumulus storm cloud.

Cirrus once meant "curl." Cirrus clouds sit very high in the sky. They look like feathery curls. These clouds can also be called "mare's tails." A mare is a female horse, and these clouds sometimes look like the tail of a running horse. You see cirrus clouds when the weather is about to change.

Flat sheets of cloud that cover the whole sky are called stratus clouds. The name *stratus* comes from the old word for "spread." These are the clouds that you often see before it rains. You may have walked through a stratus cloud. That is because these clouds sometimes lie close to the ground. When a stratus cloud is low to the ground, we call it *fog*. If you walk in the fog, you can feel how wet a cloud is. Some of the water in clouds is in the form of tiny drops, but some is in the form of a gas in the air called *water vapor*. When you see steam rising from a tea kettle, what you are seeing is vapor. As the vapor cools, it turns back into drops. When a cloud can't hold any more water, the drops will start to fall as rain, sleet, or snow. ○

172 AIM Higher! New York ELA Review

1. Who is the author of this selection?

   _____

2. What is this selection mostly about?

   _____

3. What are clouds made of?

   _____

4. How do clouds form?

   _____

5. What are three kinds of clouds?

   _____

6. What type of cloud looks like a heap of cotton?

   _____

7. What type of cloud looks like a feathery curl?

   _____

8. What type of cloud looks like a sheet spread across the sky?

   _____

9. What type of cloud do you see when the weather is fair?

   _____

10. What type of cloud do you see before it rains?

    _____

11. What is fog?

    More ▶

    _____

12. What is the name of water in gas form?

_____

Exercise C *Why can't you sit on a cloud? How can you walk through a cloud? On the lines below, write a paragraph that answers these questions. Use details from your notes in your answer.*

_____
_____
_____
_____
_____
_____
_____
_____
_____
_____
_____
_____
_____
_____

Return to the exercises at the beginning of the unit. Check your work and fix it if necessary. Give the exercises to your teacher for grading.

Unit 5
Writing Skills Review

A **writing prompt** is a short set of directions explaining what students should write about on a test. Below you can see a writing prompt and the outline one student made before he wrote his response to the prompt. You can also see the final draft of his response. Read the prompt, the student's outline, and his final draft. Then complete the exercises that follow the final draft.

Writing Prompt

Do you like hot weather or cold weather? Do you like rainy days or sunny days? Write a letter to a pen pal who lives far away. Describe your favorite kind of weather and what you like to do in this kind of weather. Use details that tell how things look, sound, feel, and even taste.

Rough Outline

Here is the outline one student made in response to the prompt. He listed the ideas he wanted to include in his letter.

Outline: A Letter to a Pen Pal

Favorite kind of weather = hot, sunny days

Favorite activity = swimming

—Ride bikes to swimming hole with my best friend & my mom

—Feel: cold water, warm sun

—Look: clear water, fish swimming

—Sound: bullfrogs making noises, kids splashing & laughing

—Taste: cold, frozen juice pops afterward

Here is the final draft the student wrote in response to the prompt. Notice how he included the ideas from his outline and connected them to each other as well as to his main idea.

One Student's Final Draft: A Letter to a Pen Pal

Dear Daniella,

    My favorite kind of weather is here. I love hot, sunny days because my favorite activity is swimming. It is great to ride bikes with my best friend and my mom to the swimming hole. The first dive in takes your breath away because the water feels so cold. The sun warms you up right away when you get out, though. The water is so clear that you can see all the fish swimming around. We always laugh when the bullfrogs make their deep, loud "vru-um" noises, trying to scare us out of their pond. Sometimes there are other kids around, and then there is a lot of splashing and laughing. Once we get back home, we cool off with icy cold frozen juice pops. That is the best part of all!

                               Your friend,
                               Sam

Your Turn

Exercise *Answer the following questions about the writing prompt and the student's response. Remember to write in complete sentences.*

1. What does the writing prompt ask the student to do? What information does the prompt ask the student to include?

   _____

   _____

   _____

   _____

   _____

2. What did the student do before writing his response?

   _____

   _____

3. Do you think that doing this was helpful? Why or why not?

   _____

   _____

4. Do you think the student will receive a good score for his response? Why or why not? (Hint: Did the student do everything the prompt asked him to do?)

   _____

   _____

   _____

   _____

   _____

Chapter 11

Step by Step

The Writing Process

In this chapter, you will learn about the writing process. A **process** has steps that happen first, second, third, and so on. Brushing your teeth is one kind of process. Even though everyone doesn't brush his or her teeth exactly the same way, the steps are generally the same. First you wet the toothbrush. Then you put toothpaste on the toothbrush. (Some people skip wetting the toothbrush or put the toothpaste on first.) Next you put the toothbrush in your mouth and brush all of your teeth in small circles. Don't forget the back teeth (as the dentist says)! After you spit out the toothpaste, you rinse your mouth with water.

Writing is another kind of process; it also involves a series of steps. Again, even though everyone doesn't follow the steps exactly the same way, the steps are generally the same.

The Writing Process

This chart shows you the five steps in the writing process:

The Writing Process

1 Prewrite

Prewriting is actually a series of steps. When you **prewrite,** you think about why you are writing. You think about who will read your piece. Next you pick a topic. Then you gather ideas and plan your writing by making an outline, a word web, a list, or a chart.

2 Draft

When you **draft,** you use the plan you made while prewriting to put your ideas into sentences on paper. This is just your first draft. If you make mistakes, you can fix them later.

3 Evaluate and Revise

When you **evaluate** your draft, you study it carefully. You look for places where your writing does not make sense. You make sure that your ideas are in order. You make sure that your writing says what you meant to say. If it needs to be improved, you **revise** it, or fix it. You look for ways to make your sentences more interesting and for words that explain and connect your ideas more clearly.

4 Proofread and Correct

The English language has many rules. When you **proofread,** you check to see that you have followed those rules. You fix any words that are not spelled or capitalized correctly. You make sure you have used commas, periods, question marks, and any other punctuation properly. You look for mistakes in grammar, such as stringy sentences and mismatched subjects (nouns) and verbs. If you see any mistakes, you **correct** them neatly.

5 Publish

After you have revised and proofread your draft or your answer, you **publish** it by sharing it with an audience. When you write for a test, you share your work with a teacher or a test-grader.

As you read on, you will see how one student went through these steps. You will see how you can use the steps in your own writing.

Prewriting

Before you write, you need to think. You need to figure out why you are going to write and what you are going to write about. Are you going to write for a class assignment or for a writing test? What exactly have you been asked to write? Who is going to read your writing? As you can see, there are many things to think about before you begin writing.

Writing for a test is different from other kinds of writing. A test gives you a **writing prompt**—a short set of directions that tell you what to write. The prompt may tell you specific things to include in your answer. It may tell you who will read your writing. When you are taking an ELA exam or any other test, the first step of prewriting is to read the prompt carefully. Then figure out exactly what the directions in the prompt are telling you to do.

Looking at the Writing Prompt

The prompt will often tell you

- the **topic** that you should write about,

- the **purpose** of your writing (such as to explain, to compare and contrast, or to describe),

- the **audience** who will read your writing,

- the **form** your writing should take (such as a letter, a paragraph, or an essay—more than one paragraph), and

- specific **details** you should include.

To do well on a test that asks you to write a response, you have to read the prompt carefully. You must understand exactly what it is asking you to do, and you must follow the directions.

Look at the sample writing prompt in the box below. The parts of this prompt are labeled to show the purpose, the audience, the form of the response, the topic, and the specific details.

Parts of a Writing Prompt

Do you like hot weather or cold weather? Do you like rainy days or sunny days?

Form   Audience

Write a letter to a pen pal who lives far

Purpose   Topic

away. Describe your favorite kind of

weather and what you like to do in this

Specific details that must

kind of weather. Use details that tell how

be included

things look, sound, feel, and taste.

The Writing Process

The **topic** is what the piece of writing should be about. The sample writing prompt asks you to write about "your favorite weather and what you like to do in this kind of weather."

The **purpose** is what the writing is supposed to accomplish: Is your answer supposed to *describe* something or to *inform* your audience about a particular subject? Does the prompt ask you to give reasons that will *persuade* your audience to believe and/or do something? Or are you supposed to *tell what happened* in a real or imaginary situation?

On a test, you can often find the purpose of your writing by looking for an action word in the prompt. In the sample prompt for the letter to a pen pal, the action word is *describe*. Notice that the prompt asks students to describe something in their own words. On the ELA exam, you will have to describe or explain something from a passage you have just read or heard. Important action words from writing prompts are shown in the chart below. Learn what these words mean. Doing so will help you to understand writing prompts on tests.

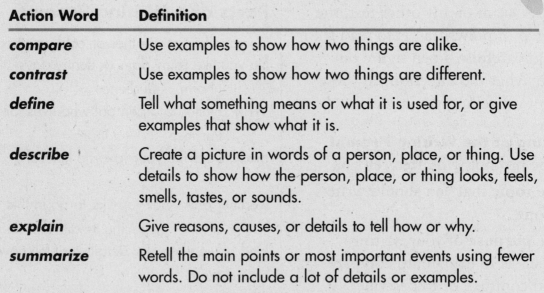

Common Action Words Used in Writing Prompts

Action Word	Definition
compare	Use examples to show how two things are alike.
contrast	Use examples to show how two things are different.
define	Tell what something means or what it is used for, or give examples that show what it is.
describe	Create a picture in words of a person, place, or thing. Use details to show how the person, place, or thing looks, feels, smells, tastes, or sounds.
explain	Give reasons, causes, or details to tell how or why.
summarize	Retell the main points or most important events using fewer words. Do not include a lot of details or examples.

Sometimes prompts will not actually use any of these words but will simply ask a question. In that case, you must decide which of these things the prompt is asking you to do.

The **form** is the type of writing you are supposed to do. The form that the writing prompt calls for in this case is a *letter*. The short-response prompts on the ELA exam will ask you to complete a chart or write a paragraph. For the extended-response prompts, you will need to write more than one paragraph.

The **audience** is the person or persons who will read the writing. The audience for the response to the sample prompt on page 181 is a *pen pal* who lives far away. Other prompts might ask you to write for a classmate, a teacher, or a relative.

Most prompts on the ELA exam do not tell who the audience for your writing is. In that case, you will write for the people who will grade the test.

You should also notice that the sample writing prompt asks you to write about specific **details.** These details include the feel, look, sound, and even taste (if possible) of your favorite weather and activity. Pay close attention to any specific details that the prompt asks you to include in your writing. The person who scores your response will be looking for these details.

How One Student Chose His Topic

To narrow his topic, first Sam thought about all the kinds of weather he likes. Then he looked over his list and thought about his favorite kind of weather and his favorite activity—swimming.

Kinds of weather I like:	What I like to do:
thunderstorms	watch from window
hot, sunny days	go swimming
first snow	make snow fort

My first choice is a hot, sunny day because I LOVE to go swimming.

The Writing Process

Choosing and Narrowing a Topic

In class, you are often given a general topic to write about that is quite broad. In this case, you have to narrow the focus of your writing to a more specific topic before you write. Before Sam wrote his letter to Daniella (see page 177), he narrowed "My Favorite Weather and Activity" to "Swimming on Hot, Sunny Days."

When you write for a class assignment, you usually have time to look for more information before choosing a specific topic. When you are writing for the ELA exam, however, you will be given topics that are already narrowed. You will not need to narrow them any further. When you are sure you know what the prompt is asking you to do, you can move right to the next step.

Finding a Main Idea

Once you have a topic, you need a main idea. Your main idea may be a one-sentence answer to a question asked in the prompt. It may be a one-sentence summary of what the prompt asks you to do. This sentence will be your topic sentence if you are writing a paragraph. All of your details will back up this main idea.

Let's look at how Sam came up with the main idea for his letter. Notice how he included that idea in his topic sentence, which is a one-sentence answer to the prompt.

How One Student Focused on a Main Idea

My narrowed topic = Swimming on hot, sunny days
(What I like to do in my favorite kind of weather)

My topic sentence:

I like different kinds of weather because you can do different things.
(<u>too broad</u>)

Last July, one day was hot and sunny and I went swimming.
(<u>too narrow</u>)

I love hot, sunny days because my favorite activity is swimming.
(<u>just right</u>)

Your Turn

Exercise Each of the following short-response prompts is based on one of the selections in the Pretest of this book. Read each prompt. Then explain the purpose of the response and write a topic sentence that answers the question in the prompt.

1. *(Based on "The Story of the House: A Chinese Folktale" on pages 3–4.)*

   Why is the young man's method for driving the others out of the house more successful than Tiger's and Dragon's methods? Use details from the story to support your answer.

   PURPOSE OF RESPONSE: _____

   _____

   TOPIC SENTENCE: _____

   _____

2. *(Based on "Tornadoes: The Most Violent Storms" on pages 10–12.)*

   What weather conditions are necessary for a tornado to form, and what are some of the signs that a tornado is coming? Use details from the article to support your answer.

   PURPOSE OF RESPONSE: _____

   _____

   TOPIC SENTENCE: _____

   _____

3. *(Based on "In the Rain Forest" on pages 15–16.)*

   In what ways do the Kayapo depend on the forest? Use details from the article to support your answer.

   PURPOSE OF RESPONSE: _____

   _____

   TOPIC SENTENCE: _____

   _____

The Writing Process

Gathering Information

Even when you understand the question (prompt) and have a good main idea, it may be hard to think of what to say. Don't panic! You can use one of these ways to get started with your writing.

Ways to Gather Information

Freewriting   When you **freewrite,** you write down whatever comes into your mind as fast as you can. Just keep writing down ideas. Do not stop to worry about whether the ideas are good ones. Afterward, you can decide which ideas are worth keeping.

Listing   Make a list of as many ideas as you can.

Word Web   In a **word web,** you start with your main idea in a circle in the middle of your paper. Then, in a cluster around this main idea, write each detail that comes to mind. Circle each detail and connect it to the main idea with a line.

Here are two ways Sam might have gathered ideas for his writing—a list and a word web.

One Student's List

"Swimming on Hot, Sunny Days"
- frozen juice pops
- bullfrogs making noises
- kids splashing & laughing
- bike riding w/best friend & my mom
- cold, clear water
- fish swimming around
- warm sun

One Student's Word Web

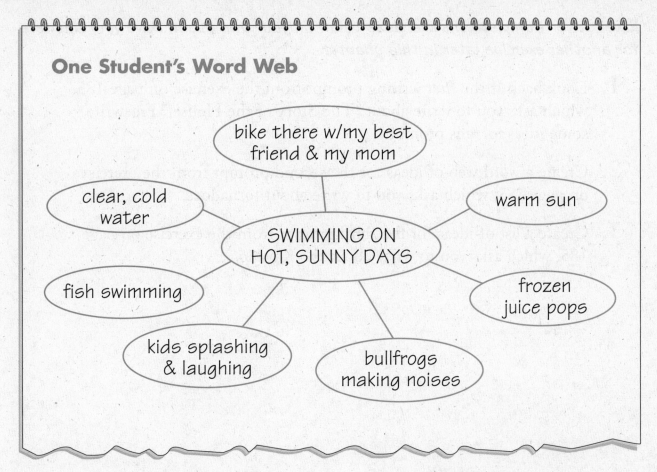

bike there w/my best friend & my mom

clear, cold water

warm sun

SWIMMING ON HOT, SUNNY DAYS

fish swimming

frozen juice pops

kids splashing & laughing

bullfrogs making noises

The two-column chart that is described in Chapter 9 on page 160 is another useful tool for gathering information. You can use such a chart to compare and contrast two people, places, or things. Before you begin prewriting, think: What details does the prompt ask me to include? Which method would be most useful for gathering these details?

Your Turn

Exercise *Complete the exercises below on your own paper. Save your answers for another exercise later in this chapter.*

1. Look back at the first writing prompt from the exercise on page 185, which asks you to write about "The Story of the House." Freewrite some ideas for this prompt.

2. Create a word web of ideas for the second prompt from the exercise on page 185, which asks you to write about tornadoes.

3. Create a list of ideas for the third prompt from the exercise on page 185, which asks you to write about the Kayapo.

The Writing Process

Organizing Your Ideas

Once you have gathered your ideas, you need to organize them. Organizing your ideas before you begin writing will help you to create a better piece of writing. Think about which method of organization would make the most sense for the type of writing you are going to do. If you are going to tell a story, you should use **chronological (time) order**: Start with what happens first. If you are going to describe something, **spatial order** might be a good choice: You can describe what you see, smell, or notice first and then zoom in for closer details. If you are going to explain the causes of an effect, you might want to tell the most important cause first, and then the next most important cause, and so on. This is **order of importance.**

If you need to **compare and contrast** two people or things, you can describe the first one completely and then explain how the second is similar to and different from the first. Or you can describe all the ways that the two people or things are alike and then tell how they are different. No matter which way you choose to organize your writing, a rough outline is a useful tool for organizing your notes.

Look back at the word web that Sam created (on page 187). Here is a rough outline that Sam made based on his word web. Notice that Sam used time order to organize his outline.

One Student's Rough Outline

Topic:
Favorite kind of weather = Hot, sunny days
Favorite activity = Swimming

Main idea: I love hot, sunny days because my favorite activity
is swimming.
—Ride bikes to swimming hole with best friend & my mom
—Feel: cold water, warm sun
—Look: clear water, fish swimming
—Sound: bullfrogs making noises, kids splashing & laughing
—Taste: cold, frozen juice pops afterward

Sam's word web was a good way to come up with ideas, but the ideas are not in any order. His rough outline is neat and organized. The prompt asked him to include details about how things look, sound, feel, and taste. His rough outline will help him to make sure he has included each one of these details in the right order. Now his letter will be much easier to write.

Your Turn

Exercise A Use the ideas from the word web below to make a rough outline. Begin by filling in the topic of the web on the line marked "Topic." Then use the information in the web to fill in the rough outline for a paragraph.

put on life jacket

learned to handle paddle

MY FIRST CANOE LESSON AT CAMP

paddled around in circle

learned to stop

TOPIC: _____

METHOD OF ORGANIZATION: _____

MAIN IDEA: _____

—DETAIL _____

—DETAIL _____

—DETAIL _____

—DETAIL _____

Exercise B Now choose the word web, freewriting, OR list that you created for the exercise on page 188 and create a rough outline on the lines provided below. You should have at least three details in your rough outline. Save your outline for another exercise later in this chapter.

TOPIC: _____

METHOD OF ORGANIZATION: _____

MAIN IDEA: _____

—DETAIL _____

—DETAIL _____

—DETAIL _____

Drafting

Once you finish prewriting, you are ready to draft. **Drafting** is putting your ideas into writing. When you write for a test, one draft may be all you have time to do. Always give yourself a few minutes at the end of the test to check your work.

Remember, if you have done a good job of prewriting, your outline will have all or most of the details you need. In the draft, you write sentences using those details. You can use words such as *first, next, then,* and *finally* to make your writing flow smoothly. A more complete list of words and phrases that connect ideas appears in Chapter 13, on page 223.

Let's look at another outline and a paragraph about a new topic. In this case, the student was asked to compare her two favorite fairytale characters. Here is the outline:

One Student's Rough Outline

My favorite fairytale characters:
—Jack from "Jack & the Beanstalk"
—Hansel from "Hansel & Gretel"
How they are alike:
   —Both start out poor & hungry
   —Both are very brave
   —Both end up happy

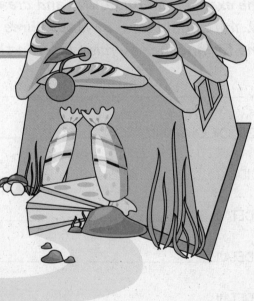

One Student's Paragraph (Rough Draft)

   Two of my favrite fairytale characters are Jack from "Jack and the Beanstalk" and Hansel from "Hansel and Gretel." They both start out very poor and do not have enough to eat. Jack and Hansel are <u>also</u> very brave. Hansel and Gretel overhere their parents saying that they are going to leave the kids in the woods. Gretel crys, <u>but</u> Hansel is brave. He stays calm and thinks of a way to get them out of the woods. Jack is brave, <u>too</u>, because he climbs very high up the beanstalk, <u>then</u> he keeps going back to the giants house, even though the giant might eat him. <u>Finally</u>, both Hansel and Jack end up happy in the end. <u>After</u> Gretel pushes the witch into the oven, Hansel and Gretel take the witch's jewels and return to their father. Jack takes all the giants treasures and lives happily with his mother. I like Jack and Hansel because they are both Brave and win in the end.

Notice the underlined words in the paragraph. These words make the connections among the ideas clear to the reader and help the writing to flow smoothly. The paragraph has a topic sentence that clearly states the main idea. The other sentences are all related to the main idea and are organized well. The student writer did exactly what the prompt asked her to do. She talked about how her favorite fairytale characters are alike. She picked three ways that they are alike and used details from the stories to support her ideas. This is an excellent draft paragraph. Notice, however, that the paragraph has some errors in grammar, punctuation, capitalization, and spelling. (Can you find them?) That is OK because this is just a draft. The writer can fix these errors later on.

Your Turn

Exercise A Use information from the short rough outline below to complete the paragraph that follows it. Fill in the blanks provided. Notice the way that the underlined words in this paragraph can help you to connect the ideas in the outline.

Main idea: The Alamo is a great place to visit.

Details: —You can walk through the historic mission church.
            —You can view a short film about the Alamo's history.
            —You can look at interesting exhibits in the museum.
            —You can walk through the beautiful gardens.

The Alamo in San Antonio, Texas, _____

_____ .

You can <u>begin</u> your visit by _____

_____ .

<u>Next</u>, you can _____

about the Battle of the Alamo in 1836. <u>After that</u>, it is interesting

to see _____ .

You can <u>also</u> enjoy _____ .

The Alamo is a wonderful place for people who like history.

Exercise B Look back at the rough outline that you created for Exercise B on page 191. Use the outline to write a rough draft of a paragraph on your own paper. Add words to connect your ideas, as shown in the sample draft paragraph on page 193. Save your draft for another exercise later in this chapter.

The Writing Process

Evaluating and Revising

Once you have done your prewriting and written a draft, the next step in the writing process is evaluating and revising. **Evaluating** means checking over what you have written. In this step, you decide what changes to make to improve your draft. **Revising** means making those changes. You might change the order of ideas. You might think of better words to use. You might add some details or cross out details that do not belong.

When you write for a test, you may not have time to write a final draft. Therefore, you should write your first draft as carefully as possible, but always leave a little bit of time to check your work and revise it. You can make changes neatly right on your first draft. Your grade will be lower if you make mistakes. It is important to correct as many mistakes as possible before you hand in your test.

Use the checklist on the next page to evaluate and revise your writing. As you revise, you can do four things:

- You can add new material:

  the hill
  Jack and Jill fell down.
                        ∧

- You can remove material:

  Jack and Jill fell ~~down.~~

- You can move material:

  Jill fell down (also)

- You can change (or reword) material:

  but did not get hurt
  Jack and Jill fell down ~~the hill~~.
                          ∧

Notice how the words that are crossed out in the examples above are crossed out with a single line. Each word or phrase that is added is written neatly above the line where it is supposed to go. When you make corrections to your draft, always make them as neatly as possible.

Revision Checklist

Questions to Ask about Any Piece of Writing

✔ **Check the Audience:**

❑ Is the piece written in a style that fits the audience?

❑ Will the audience understand the words that are used?

✔ **Check the Purpose:**

❑ Does the writing answer the test prompt completely?
(if you are writing for a test)

❑ Does the writing accomplish its purpose (for example, to persuade, inform, describe, or entertain)?

✔ **Check the Style and Voice:**

❑ Does the writing use the right words to express each idea?

❑ Do the sentences vary in length?

❑ Is the writing interesting to read?

✔ **Check the Structure and Organization:**

❑ Does each paragraph have a topic sentence?

❑ Are all the important details included?

❑ Are the ideas in an order that makes sense?

❑ Are the connections between ideas clear?

✔ **Check the Focus and Supporting Details:**

❑ Is the main idea clear?

❑ Does every sentence in the paragraph support the topic sentence?

❑ Are there any sentences that do not belong?

❑ Are there enough details to support the idea in the topic sentence?

Let's look at how Sam revised the first draft of his letter to Daniella:

Sam's Rough Draft

Dear Daniella,

My favorite kind of weather is here. I love hot,

because

sunny days. My favorite activity is swimming.

_m_

It is great to ride bikes to the swiming hole

with my best friend and my mom. The first

_in_

dive takes your breath away because the

that

water feels so cold. The water is clear ~~so~~ you

_m_

can see all the fish swiming around. The sun

warms you up right away when you get out,

_h_

tough. We always laugh when the bullfrogs

deep, loud "vru-um"

make their noises, trying to scare us out of

their pond. Sometimes there are other kids

and then there is a lot of splashing and laughing.

around, ~~too~~. Once we get back home ~~on Oak~~

~~Street~~, we cool off with icy cold frozen juice

pops. That is the best part of all!

Your friend,
Sam

Why Sam Changed It

—Combining the second and third sentences gives my letter a clear main idea.

—Moving up the sentence about the sun makes more sense (after I say how cold the water is).

—I added these words to try to tell what sound the frogs make. I also needed to add what it sounds like when there are lots of kids around.

—I did not need the detail about the name of the street where I live, so I took it out.

Exercise Evaluate and revise the paragraph that you created for Exercise B on page 194. Use the Revision Checklist on page 196 to review your first draft. Then write your revised draft on the lines provided below. Use additional paper if necessary. Save your revised draft for another exercise at the end of this chapter.

The Writing Process

Proofreading

The next step in the writing process is proofreading. **Proofreading** means correcting mistakes in grammar, usage, capitalization, punctuation, and spelling. Even if you write a clever, exciting piece, mistakes of this kind can make it impossible to read.

Here is a helpful checklist to use when you proofread your writing:

Proofreading Checklist

✔ **Form**
- ❏ Every paragraph is indented.
- ❏ There are margins on both sides.
- ❏ The handwriting is clear.

✔ **Grammar and Usage**
- ❏ Each sentence has a subject (noun) and a predicate (verb).
- ❏ If the subject is singular (only one person doing the action), so is the verb.
- ❏ If the subject is plural (more than one person doing the action), so is the verb.
- ❏ The right words are used to describe or explain ideas.
- ❏ There are no run-on sentences.

✔ **Spelling**
- ❏ All words, including names, are spelled correctly.

✔ **Capitalization**
- ❏ Every sentence begins with a capital letter.
- ❏ All names of specific people and places are capitalized.

✔ **Punctuation**
- ❏ Every sentence has an end mark—a period (.), an exclamation point (!), or a question mark (?).
- ❏ Commas are used correctly.
- ❏ All quotations are in quotation marks.

The Writing Process

When you proofread, make your corrections as neatly as possible. For example, do not scratch out a word and scribble a replacement above it. Instead, draw a single line through the word you want to replace. Then write in the new word neatly. If you want to change a lowercase letter (such as *s* or *d*) to a capital letter (such as *S* or *D*), do not simply write the capital letter on top of the lowercase letter. Instead, draw three lines under the lowercase letter to show that it should be capitalized. Here are some other proofreading marks that will be useful to you:

Revision and Proofreading Symbols

Proofreading Mark	Meaning
mountain a red bike ^	Add something that is missing.
a really hard problem	Take out letters or words.
a wierd sound	Switch the order of letters or words.
some thing great	Close up space.
panda#bear	Add a space.
the harvest Moon	Make lowercase.
President adams	Capitalize.
storm. ¶ Later,	Begin a new paragraph.
Step this way ⊙	Add a period.
boats, cars and planes	Add a comma.
dumb a dum idea	Change a word or phrase; correct a spelling

Your Turn

Exercise A *Rewrite the following sentences. Make all the corrections shown by the proofreading marks.*

1. some scientists think that one day, people will live on mars⊙

   _____

   _____

2. It was a dark and storm y night.

   _____

   _____

3. Let's keep this a secret be tween you and I.

   _____

   _____

4. The space shuttle will take of at 3:00.

   _____

   _____

5. Thier bookbags are on in there lokers⊙

   _____

   _____

6. Frederick douglass founded a newspaper in boston.

   _____

   _____

7. Where in the World are you?

   _____

   _____

More ▶

Your Turn

Exercise B *Use proofreading marks to correct the errors in the paragraph below. The corrections you should make to each sentence are listed (marked with matching letters) at the bottom of the page.*

a. Long ago, on an island in the south pacific, their lived a boy named pali. b. he was an excellent swimmer and he loved to dive under the water to see the treasures there. c. One day, while diving, Pali found a botle. d. In side was a note. e. Pali could not read the note because it was written in a forein language. f. So, Pali took the note to his Friend, William Thorndike, an old sea captain who had seen many lands. g. William read the note, which was writen in english. It said:

> My boat is sinking, and I know not if I shall
> survive. If you are reading this, thank your stars,
> for you are probably better off than I am.
> Peace to you, and to all good men and women.
> —Captain William Thorndike

a. Begin with a paragraph indent.
Capitalize *South* and *Pacific*.
Change *their* to *there*.
Capitalize *Pali*.

b. Begin with a capital letter.
Add a comma after *swimmer*.

c. Change *botle* to *bottle*.

d. Close up the space between *In* and *side*.

e. Change *forein* to *foreign*.

f. Make the *f* in *friend* lowercase.

g. Change the word *read* to *translated*.
Correct the spelling of the word *written*.
Capitalize the first letter in the word *English*.

The Writing Process

Remember, you will probably not have time to make a final copy of your paragraph or essay during a test. You may need to make your corrections right on your draft.

How to Write Answers for Tests

- **Prewriting:** Read the prompt carefully. Gather ideas. Then put your ideas in a rough outline.

- **Drafting:** Use your outline to write a first draft. Do not worry too much about making mistakes at this point. Follow the organization in your outline.

- **Evaluating and Revising:** Reread your draft. Look for places where you might add, remove, move, or change words, phrases, or sentences to make your writing better.

- **Proofreading and Correcting:** Read your response one more time. Fix any mistakes in spelling, punctuation, capitalization, grammar, and choice of words.

Using this process whenever you take a writing test will help you to do the best job you can.

Publishing or Sharing

When you are writing for a test, **publishing,** or sharing, your work is easy. You simply turn in your test! When you are writing on your own, here are some other ways to share your work:

Publishing or Sharing Written Work

- Put it on a bulletin board.
- Make a booklet or scrapbook.
- Read it aloud.
- Show it to a friend, classmate, or relative.
- Send it to a newspaper.

Your Turn

Exercise Now that you know how to use proofreading marks, use the Proofreading Checklist on page 199 to check the draft you revised on page 198. Check for errors in form, grammar, spelling, capitalization, and punctuation. Make corrections as neatly as possible. Then make a clean final copy on the lines provided below, and share it with your classmates.

_____

_____

_____

_____

_____

_____

_____

_____

_____

_____

_____

_____

_____

_____

_____

Chapter 12

Sentence Sense

Building Strong Sentences

Writing Complete Sentences

Good writing uses clear, well-built sentences. This means that the sentences have all the right parts in all the right places. Every sentence must have a subject and a **predicate** (a verb or verb phrase). The **subject** tells *who* or *what* is doing (or involved in) the action in the sentence. Remember that the subject is usually a noun or a pronoun. The other part that is required to create a complete sentence is a verb or verb phrase. The subject and the verb are the building blocks of the sentence. Without these two pieces, a sentence is not complete.

Correcting Fragments

Sometimes when people talk to each other, they do not use complete sentences. Suppose that your friend Carlos asks you, "Did you go to that movie we talked about?" You reply, "Yeah. Funny." Carlos knows what you mean, since he knows the question he asked you. If Carlos's dad walked into the room as you gave your answer, however, he would *not* know what you are talking about. This is because your answer is a fragment. It only gives half a

thought: *something* was funny, but what? Your reply does not tell the listener what that *something* was. The subject (in this case, the movie) is missing in your response to Carlos.

When you review your writing, take a close look at each of your sentences. Be sure that each sentence is a complete thought, with a subject that tells *who* or *what* and a **verb** that tells what the subject *is* or *does*. Also check that each sentence can stand alone and be understood by itself. If a sentence is missing either a subject or a verb, it is a **fragment.** To make the sentence complete, you will need to add the missing piece. See if you can tell what is missing in the fragment below.

FRAGMENT: Waited in line at the food stand.

COMPLETE SENTENCE: **The fans** waited in line at the food stand.

The fragment does not tell *who* or *what* waited in line. The complete sentence contains the subject *fans*.

Your Turn

Exercise The following paragraph about cave animals has some complete sentences and some fragments. Some sentences are missing the subject (who or what). Some are missing the predicate (the verb part). You will find the missing subjects and predicates in the box below the paragraph. Use the words and phrases from the box to fill in the missing pieces in the sentence fragments. Rewrite the paragraph on the lines below the box.

Spend their whole lives in dark caves. The scientific term for these animals is *troglodytes,* which means "cave dwellers." Because they live in the dark, these unusual animals look different from other animals. The Ozark cavefish. Some cave-dwelling salamanders. Do not have pigment in their skin. Instead of having normal coloring, they. Should go visit a cave and see these cave dwellers for yourself.

Subjects	Predicates (Verb Phrases)
They	look white.
You	does not have eyes.
Some animals	are albino.

EXAMPLE: Some animals spend their whole lives in dark caves.

_____

_____

_____

_____

_____

_____

_____

Building Strong Sentences

Using a Variety of Sentence Types

Good writing involves more than fixing fragments. In addition, good writing includes sentences of different types. Suppose that a television show had characters who all dressed the same and talked the same way. The show would be pretty boring. In the same way, writing that uses one type of sentence over and over is boring, too. In this section, you will learn how to use different sentence types.

There are four types of sentence: statements, questions, exclamations, and commands. As you will see in the following examples, each type of sentence is put together in a different way. Each sentence type also requires its own type of punctuation mark.

Statements

The type of sentence you will see most often is a statement. A **statement** is a sentence that tells something about a person, place, or thing. It ends with a period (.). Read these two statements:

The Appalachian Mountains run through the eastern United States.

The tallest mountain in the eastern United States is Mount Mitchell.

In a statement, the subject of the sentence usually comes before the verb. In the first sentence above, *Appalachian Mountains* is the subject. It comes before the verb *run*.

subject *verb*
The Appalachian Mountains run | *predicate*
through the eastern United States.

In the second sentence, *mountain* is the subject. It comes before the verb *is*.

subject
The tallest mountain in the eastern United States is Mount | *predicate*
Mitchell. *verb*

Questions

Another common type of sentence is a question. A **question** asks something. It ends with a question mark (?).

Where are the Appalachian Mountains? *verb* *subject*

What is the tallest mountain in the eastern United States?

In a question, the subject usually comes after the verb. For example, in the first sentence in the pair above, the subject is *Appalachian Mountains*. Notice that in this case, the subject comes after the verb *are*. In the second sentence, the subject *mountain* comes after the verb *is*.

Exclamations

A third type of sentence is an exclamation. An **exclamation** expresses a strong or sudden feeling. It ends with an exclamation point (!).

I love the mountains!

Let's go for a hike!

In an exclamation, the subject usually comes before the verb. In the first example, the subject *I* comes before the verb *love*. Sometimes, in an exclamation, the subject is **implied.** This means that the subject does not appear in the sentence but is understood. In the second example above, *you* is the implied subject, and *let* is the verb.

Commands

The fourth type of sentence is a command. A **command** asks or tells someone to do something. Like a statement, a command usually ends with a period.

Please find Mount Mitchell on this map.

Do not climb too high up the trail by yourself.

In commands, the subject is often implied. It is usually understood to be *you*. This is the case in both sentences in the pair above. In the first sentence, the subject is *you*, and the verb is *find.*

verb

Please **find** Mount Mitchell on this map.

In the second sentence, the subject is *you*, and the verbs are *do* and *climb.*

verb

Do not **climb** too high up the trail by yourself.

Sometimes a command ends with an exclamation point instead of a period. For example, if your teacher wants you to sit down, he or she might say:

Please sit down.

Here the command ends with a period. If your teacher has to tell you a second, third, or fourth time, however, he or she might say:

Sit down, now!

The exclamation point shows that this command is said with strong feeling.

When you write, use more than one sentence type. Using different kinds of sentences will help to make your writing more interesting.

Read the following paragraph by a student named Elisa. In her first draft, Elisa did not use different types of sentence. There is not much variety in her writing.

One Student's Paragraph (Elisa's First Draft)

Hoover Dam is one of the biggest dams in the world. I went to Hoover Dam last summer with my aunt and uncle. The day we went was very hot. It was over 100 degrees. The best part of the tour was walking on top of the dam. You could see Lake Mead stretching for miles on one side. The dam wall dropped hundreds of feet down into Boulder Canyon on the other side. You could walk from one state to another on top of the dam. On one side was Nevada. On the other side was Arizona. Hoover Dam is great. You should go there.

Did you notice that almost all the sentences in this first draft are statements? Now, look what happens when Elisa changes some of her sentences to other types.

Elisa's Revised Draft

Did you know that Hoover Dam is one of the biggest dams in — **question**
the world? Last summer, I was lucky enough to take a trip there
with my aunt and uncle. It was over 100 degrees on the day we
arrived. We took a walking tour across the top of the dam to — **statements**
see the view. On one side, the waters of Lake Mead stretch for
miles. On the other side, the dam wall drops hundreds of feet
down into Boulder Canyon. The dam is huge! We walked from one
end of the dam to the other. That walk took us from Nevada to — **exclamations**
Arizona! Try to visit Hoover Dam someday. The beautiful view and
the size of the dam may surprise you!

command

When she revised her paragraph, Elisa made sure to have a variety of sentence types in her paragraph. She also made a few other changes to help the paragraph flow more smoothly and make it more interesting. She rewrote the first sentence as a question. This helps get the reader interested in the topic. Then she changed the words in the second sentence so that it would tell how she felt about the trip. Elisa combined the ideas in her third and fourth sentences to create a longer sentence that is less choppy. She added a sentence about the tour to help the reader better understand the order of events. She also combined the two separate sentences about the views on both sides of the dam into a single sentence. Elisa did this by putting a comma (,) and the word *and* between the related parts of the original sentences. She also made the capital letter that was at the beginning of the second sentence lower case. Finally, she turned her next to the last sentence into a command. She ended her paragraph with an exclamation, to share with her reader the excitement she felt about seeing the dam. Elisa's changes make her paragraph more interesting to read.

Your Turn

Exercise A *Each of the following sentences is labeled according to its type. On the line below each sentence, follow the directions to rewrite it as another type of sentence. The first example has been done for you.*

EXAMPLE: There are fish in that cave. (statement)

Change this to a question:

<u>Are there fish in that cave?</u>

1. Turn off your flashlight! (command)

   Change this to a question:

   _____

2. Do some bats live in caves? (question)

   Change this to a statement:

   _____

3. It is getting chilly in here. (statement)

   Change this to a question:

   _____

4. I see the way out of the cave. (statement)

   Change this to an exclamation:

   _____

5. Could you give me your rope? (question)

   Change this to a command:

   _____

More ▶

Your Turn

Exercise B All the sentences in the following paragraph are statements. Improve the paragraph by changing some of the sentences to different types. The directions in parentheses tell you how to change each numbered sentence. Write the new sentences on the lines provided below.

[1]Carlsbad Caverns National Park has more than ninety caves. **(Change this to an exclamation.)** The caves sink down as far as 1,567 feet below the Earth's surface. An elevator goes down into one of the caves. [2]You probably have never eaten in an underground cafeteria. **(Change this to a question.)** This cave has a place where hungry visitors can get a snack. Other caves are much harder to get to. You have to go with a guide and take a flashlight. [3]You might even have to crawl and squeeze through narrow passages. **(Change this to an exclamation.)** Either way, there is plenty to see for everyone who comes. [4]You can go see the caves for yourself if you want. **(Change this to a command.)**

1. _____

_____

2. _____

_____

3. _____

_____

4. _____

_____

Building Strong Sentences

Combining and Expanding Sentences

The easiest kind of sentence to write is a simple sentence. **Simple sentences** have one subject and one verb.[1] Each simple sentence expresses one complete thought. Writing that uses only simple sentences often sounds . . . well, simple. A whole paragraph of simple sentences can get pretty boring.

Combining Sentences

Not only is a paragraph of simple sentences boring, it is also choppy. Read the following paragraph by a student named Ryan. It is made up of simple sentences. Notice how the paragraph sounds choppy. The sentences are all the same length, and Ryan repeats the same subject over and over.

One Student's Paragraph (Ryan's First Draft)

The planet Saturn is famous for its rings. Other planets also have rings. None of them is as beautiful as Saturn. You can look at Saturn through a telescope. You can see what looks like several golden rings. Each "ring" is made up of thousands of tiny ringlets. The first person to see the rings thought they were solid. The rings are really made of millions of pieces of ice. Some of these pieces are as small as dust. Others are more than ten feet across. Saturn's rings make it one of the most beautiful planets.

Ryan decided that he did not like the way his paragraph sounded, so he decided to combine some of the sentences. Read the revised version of his paragraph below. The changes are underlined. See if you can explain why Ryan made them.

Ryan's Revised Paragraph

The planet Saturn is famous for its rings. <u>There are other planets with rings, but none of them is as beautiful as Saturn. If you look at Saturn through a telescope, you can see what looks like several golden rings.</u> Each "ring" is made up of thousands of tiny ringlets. <u>The first person to see the rings thought they were solid, but the rings are really made of millions of pieces of ice. Some of these pieces are as small as dust, and others are more than ten feet across.</u> Saturn's rings make it one of the most beautiful planets.

---

[1]Each part may, however, be compound, as in the simple sentence *Jack and Jill tripped and fell.*

You have already seen that good writing uses sentences of different types. Now you can see that it also uses sentences of different lengths.

Try reading your writing out loud. If your writing sounds choppy, one way you can fix it is to combine some of the sentences. Sometimes you can combine two related sentences into one compound sentence. A **compound sentence** is a sentence that contains two complete thoughts. The thoughts are connected with a comma and a conjunction.

Notice how these two sentences express two complete thoughts:

> *verb*
> The children **walked** to the pond.
> *subject* *predicate*
> The ducks **swam** over to them.
> *verb*

Each of these sentences has a subject and a verb. In the combined version below, the comma and the word *and* join the two thoughts into one compound sentence. Words such as *and* that join two complete thoughts are called **conjunctions.**

> *conjunction*
> The children walked to the pond, **and** the ducks swam over to them.

Sometimes you can combine parts of a sentence. Read these sentences:

> The children **were** noisy.
> *subject* *verb phrase*
> The children **were** happy.

Both sentences have the same subject. Instead of repeating the subject, you can just combine the verb phrases. A **phrase** is a group of words in a sentence that expresses only part of a thought. A **verb phrase** is the verb and the rest of the words that come after the verb. (This part of the sentence is also called the predicate.)

> *subject* *verb phrase (predicate)*
> The children **were** noisy and happy.
> *verb*

Notice that a sentence with a combined verb phrase is not the same thing as a compound sentence.

The subjects of sentences can also sometimes be combined.

> Kim **fed** the ducks.
> *subjects* *verb phrase*
> Peter **fed** the ducks.

The verb phrase in both of the sentences is the same. So, the subjects can be combined.

> *subject* *verb phrase (predicate)*
> Kim and Peter **fed** the ducks.

Coordinating conjunctions join the parts of sentences. This box lists five coordinating conjunctions:

and	but	or	so	yet

The sentences in the pairs below can all be combined in some way. In these examples, a conjunction other than *and* is used to combine each pair of sentences.

1. Use a compound subject. (Combine the subjects.)

Dina might bike around the lake.   + Marty might bike around the lake.

compound subject   **predicate**

Dina **or** Marty might bike around the lake.

↖conjunction

2. Use a compound predicate, or verb phrase. (Combine the verb phrases.)

Jessie can feed the ducks.   + Jessie cannot swim.

compound predicate

Jessie can feed the ducks **but** cannot swim.

↖conjunction

3. Use a compound sentence. (Combine the complete thoughts.)

The ducks are swimming away.   + The kids cannot feed them anymore.

subject   **predicate**   **subject**   **predicate**

The ducks are swimming away, **so** the kids cannot feed them anymore.

↖conjunction

The sign says "Keep off the grass." + I see someone walking across the yard.

subject   **predicate**   **subject**   **predicate**

The sign says " Keep off the grass," **yet** I see someone walking across the yard.

↖conjunction

When you write a compound sentence, remember to use a comma before the conjunction to link the complete thoughts. When you combine parts only (either two subjects or two verbs), in a compound subject or a compound verb phrase, do *not* use a comma before the conjunction.

compound subject   **compound predicate**

INCORRECT: Dina, or Marty might bike around the lake, or feed the ducks.

Your Turn

Exercise *The following paragraph does not flow well because it is full of short, choppy sentences. Some sentences need to be combined. Use conjunctions such as* and, or, but, *or* so *to combine the sentences in color. Write your new complete sentences on the lines provided below. In each new sentence, circle the conjunction you used to connect the thoughts. An example has been provided for you.*

EXAMPLE: I wanted to look at Saturn. We looked at the moon first.

I wanted to look at Saturn, (but) we looked at the moon first.

Last Saturday night, I got to look through a telescope. [1]A friend of my mom's has a pretty powerful telescope. She let us borrow it. We set it up in the middle of a field while the sun was setting. [2]Then we waited until it got dark. We could start looking around. I wanted to look at Saturn, but we looked at the moon first. It was amazing to see all the bumps and craters on the moon's surface. Then, we looked at planets. Mars was small and red, just as I thought it would be. Saturn was beautiful. [3]I could see the rings around it. There were a couple of moons off to one side. I cannot wait to get another look through the telescope.

1. _____

_____

2. _____

_____

3. _____

_____

Correcting Run-Ons

The conjunction is a *very* important part of a compound sentence. Sometimes people forget this. Instead, they make the mistake of combining two complete sentences by simply changing the period between the parts to a comma. This turns the sentences into a run-on. Run-ons are always incorrect.

A **run-on** is two or more complete sentences that have been combined without a conjunction. A run-on is a sentence error. Avoid this type of mistake. When you combine separate sentences, use a comma but don't forget to add a conjunction, too. (See the compound sentence about soccer and basketball below.)

Look carefully for run-ons when you revise your writing. If you find two complete thoughts with no conjunction between them, you have found a run-on. There are two ways to fix a run-on: You can add a comma and a conjunction, or you can turn the run-on sentence into two separate sentences. Study these examples:

RUN-ON SENTENCE:
(incorrect)
Soccer is my favorite sport, basketball is fun, too.

comma

COMPOUND SENTENCE:
(correct)
Soccer is my favorite sport, **but** basketball is fun, too.

conjunction

TWO SENTENCES:
(also correct)
Soccer is my favorite sport. Basketball is fun, too.

period

Your Turn

Exercise *Read the following sentences. Decide whether each numbered sentence below is a run-on or a correct sentence. To help figure this out, look for a conjunction between the two complete thoughts. If the sentence has a conjunction, circle it and write "correct" on the blank following the sentence. If the sentence does not have a conjunction, write "run-on" on the line.*

EXAMPLE: We drove to the beach, (and) I swam in the ocean.

correct

1. The waves were big, they almost knocked me over.

   _____

2. I got tired of swimming, so I sat on the beach.

   _____

3. It was a sunny day, the sand felt really hot.

   _____

4. We brought an umbrella to sit under, we still got pretty warm.

   _____

5. My dad fixed us lunch, and we ate at a picnic table.

   _____

Building Strong Sentences

Reviewing Your Writing

You want to be sure that readers will understand and enjoy what you write. So, when you review your writing, there are several things you should check:

Sentence Checklist

☐ Read each sentence to make sure it expresses a complete thought. Does it have both a subject and a predicate (verb or verb phrase)?

☐ Watch for fragments. If you find a fragment, decide which part of the sentence (subject or verb?) is missing. Add that part to the sentence.

☐ Watch for run-ons. Remember that if you discover a run-on, you can correct it in two ways: You can add a comma and a conjunction, or you can write two or more separate sentences.

If you notice that your writing sounds choppy or does not flow well, try some of the following ways to revise your sentences:

Ways to Improve Your Sentences

✔ **Change your sentence types for variety.** Remember that you can sometimes change one type of sentence to another. For example, you can often turn a statement into a question, and you can often turn a question into a command.

✔ **Combine your sentences for smoother flow.** You can use a comma and a conjunction to join two related sentences into a compound sentence. Also, you can often combine verb phrases in sentences that have the same subject. Another way to combine sentences is to combine subjects that share the same verb phrase.

Your Turn

Exercise A *Follow the directions to revise the paragraph below.*

1. Read the paragraph about meerkats. As you read it the first time, think about the changes you would like to make.

2. Read the paragraph again. This time, use proofreading marks to mark changes you would like to make in the paragraph. Make sure the sentences are varied. Make sure there are no sentence fragments or run-ons.

> This is what meerkats are. They are animals that live in southern Africa. Meerkats are small. Meerkats are fast. They live together in large groups, the adults work together to take care of the young meerkats. Meerkats are pretty good about sharing space with each other. Sometimes, meerkats share their tunnels with ground squirrels. Meerkats have long bodies. And long tails for balance, to help them stand and look around. Helps them keep an eye out for danger. Meerkats eat insects. Meerkats eat snakes. Meerkats also eat other things. You can look for meerkats the next time you go to the zoo.

Exercise B *Using the improvements you have made, write a clean revised draft of the paragraph about meerkats on the lines provided below.*

_____

_____

_____

_____

_____

_____

_____

_____

_____

_____

_____

_____

_____

_____

_____

_____

Chapter 13

Perfect Paragraphs

Main Ideas and Supporting Details

Some questions on the ELA exam will ask you to write short responses. Often, you will be able to answer a question in a couple of sentences. Sometimes, however, you will need to write a paragraph or more. The extended-response items on the exam will usually require more than one paragraph. In this chapter, you will learn how to write paragraphs that are strong enough to serve as answers on tests.

What Is a Paragraph?

A **paragraph** is a group of sentences about a single main idea. Here is a paragraph about bats:

There is one thing that makes bats different from other mammals: Bats can fly. Bats do not have feathers, and bat wings are different from bird wings. In fact, bat wings are a lot like the human hand. Each wing has an arm, four long fingers, and a short thumb. Very thin skin stretches between the fingers. The thumb and each finger can move. This is how the bat changes the shape of its wings. The shape of the bat's

wings helps it change direction. In a split second, a bat can turn, roll, and swoop. These are the skills it needs to catch fast-flying insects. In one hour, a bat can catch more than a hundred bugs! The bat's ability to fly makes it a very special animal indeed.

The paragraph has three parts—a topic sentence, supporting sentences, and a clincher sentence.

The first sentence is the **topic sentence.** It tells the main idea of the paragraph.

The last sentence is the clincher sentence. The **clincher sentence** is a **concluding sentence** that reinforces the main idea of the paragraph. It sums up the author's point and often restates the main idea in different words.

The sentences between the topic sentence and the concluding sentence are **supporting sentences.** These sentences give facts and details to support the topic sentence.

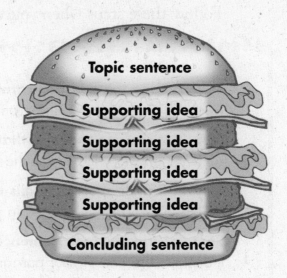

Topic sentence

Supporting idea

Supporting idea

Supporting idea

Supporting idea

Concluding sentence

You can think of a paragraph as being like a cheeseburger. The topic sentence is the bun on top. The concluding sentence is the bun at the bottom. The burger, lettuce, and cheese in the middle are the supporting sentences that give facts and details or examples.

Connecting Ideas in a Paragraph

In a paragraph, the supporting ideas should all be related to the main idea. The sentences about supporting details should also be connected to each other. Use words and phrases such as the ones listed below to make clear connections between the ideas in each paragraph you write.

Words That Connect Ideas

for example	also	across	but
first	later	below	because
second	before	in front	one kind
next	next to	behind	another kind
then	above	too	therefore

Main Ideas and Supporting Details

Follow these steps when you write a paragraph for a test:

Step 1: Read the question carefully. Make sure that you understand what the question or writing prompt is asking you to do.

Step 2: Write one sentence that answers the question. This one-sentence answer will become the topic sentence of your paragraph.

Step 3: Gather specific details to support your answer. These details should back up the main idea in your topic sentence.

Step 4: Write the topic sentence and the supporting sentences. Indent the first line of your paragraph. On a test, it is usually best to start your paragraph with your topic sentence and then move on to the details of your answer. Be sure to use complete sentences. In your supporting sentences, give details and examples that explain the main idea. Use words like *first, second, then,* and *next* to show how your ideas are connected to each other. Also, make sure that all your ideas are related to the main idea.

Step 5: Write a clincher sentence for your paragraph. The clincher sentence is your concluding sentence. It should strongly support your main idea by explaining it in different words.

Step 6: Check your paragraph. Look at your sentences. Did you say all you wanted to? Did you go off track and bring in extra details that are not related to your main idea? Look for mistakes.

- Did you indent your first sentence?
- Did you spell each word correctly?
- Did you use a capital letter at the beginning of each sentence?
- Did you use a capital letter at the beginning of each name of a person or place?
- Did you use a period, question mark, or exclamation mark at the end of each sentence?

Correct your paper neatly.

A paragraph answer should look like the one below. The paragraph has a topic sentence, supporting sentences with specific details, and a concluding sentence. The concluding sentence restates the main idea of the topic sentence but in different words.

Sample Writing Prompt and Answer

Is "The Story of the House" about real characters and events or about imaginary ones? Explain. Use specific details from the story to support your response.

The question in this prompt is based on the Chinese folktale on pages 3–4 about the three beings who lived after the storm. Here is how one student answered the prompt. Read this paragraph. Then answer the questions about it on the next page.

One Student's Response

"The Story of the House" is about imaginary characters and events. In this story, Dragon and Tiger talk and act like people and live in a house with a man. A dragon is an imaginary animal. A tiger is a real animal, but it does not talk. In real life, the tiger would probably attack the man. Also, Tiger and Dragon have special powers. Tiger's roar moves trees and rocks. Dragon can create a big storm. Another clue that this story is imaginary is in the title. It says, "A Chinese Folktale"! Most folktales, like "Jack and the Beanstalk," are about made-up characters and events.

Exercise A *Answer these questions about the sample paragraph-length response you just read. Write your answers in complete sentences. Remember to put quotation marks around any words or sentences that you repeat word for word from the sample response.*

1. What is the **topic sentence** of the paragraph—the one that gives the main idea?

   _____

   _____

2. What are three words in the paragraph that show how the ideas are connected? (See the list of **connecting words** on page 223.)

   _____

   _____

3. Which sentence is the **clincher sentence**—the one that sums up the main idea?

   _____

   _____

Exercise B *Fill in the blanks with words that connect the sentences. Use connecting words from the list on page 223.*

1. This is my street. On the corner is my house. _____ to it live the Bernsteins. _____ the street live the Guptas.

2. First, we felt the cold wind. _____, we saw the dark clouds. We knew it was going to rain.

3. Bears live in many of different kinds of homes. _____, they live in bamboo forests, on Arctic ice floes, and in the rain forests of Asia.

4. Making hot cocoa is simple. _____, warm the milk in a pan. _____, put two teaspoons of cocoa in a cup. _____, pour the warm milk into the cup and stir. Now, enjoy!

Exercise C *Choose ONE of the topics listed below. Then write a topic sentence that tells the main idea of a paragraph that you could write about your topic.*

—Your favorite movie
—Ice cream
—Snakes

YOUR TOPIC: _____

_____

YOUR TOPIC SENTENCE: _____

_____

_____

Your Turn

Exercise D *On the lines provided below, write a paragraph describing a funny thing that happened to you or to someone you know. Write about what happened* first, next, *and* last. *Use these or other connecting words from the chart on page 223.*

_____

_____

_____

_____

_____

_____

_____

_____

_____

_____

_____

_____

_____

_____

_____

_____

_____

Chapter 14

Excellent Essays

Introduction, Body, and Conclusion

Sometimes you will be asked to write more than one paragraph about a single topic. A piece of nonfiction writing that is longer than a single paragraph is called an **essay.**

Not all essays are alike, but most will have the same parts: an introduction, a body of text about the topic, and a conclusion.

Read the following student essay about alligator holes.

Parts of an Essay

An essay has three main parts:

1. The **introduction** is a paragraph that catches the reader's attention. It also tells the main idea, or **thesis,** of the essay.

2. The **body** presents ideas that support the thesis. The body can be one or more paragraphs long.

3. The **conclusion** is a paragraph that sums up the ideas in the rest of the essay.

One Student's Essay   Jenna Liu

Would You Swim in an Alligator Hole?

Did you know that people are not the only creatures who go swimming to cool off on hot days? Alligators, like other reptiles, need a place to stay cool when the weather is hot. The alligators that live in the Florida Everglades survive the dry season by digging swimming holes. The alligators are not the only ones to use the holes. By making sure that there is a source of water throughout the dry season, alligators in the Everglades help many other animals and plants to survive.

introduction

More ▶

Introduction, Body, and Conclusion

The Everglades is sometimes called a "river of grass." During the wet season, the grassy marshes are flooded with water. When the rainy season ends in October, the wet grasslands start to dry up. Then the alligator goes to work. Using its powerful legs, it pushes aside plants and dirt to make a hole in the ground. This 'gator hole becomes a little pond that holds water longer than the dry ground around it. The alligator now has a place where it can stay wet and cool.

body

Other animals, such as fish, frogs, birds, and turtles, visit the alligator's new pond. Some come to eat snails and small creatures that live in the water. Others come for a cool drink or to lay eggs in or near the pond. Some of these visitors become the alligator's dinner. However, many other animals are able to survive the dry season because of the water the alligator has provided.

Plants benefit from the alligator hole, too. Lily pads float on top. Water plants grow near the edges of the hole. A little farther away, ferns, willow trees, and other plants that like to have "wet feet" grow in the mounds of dirt around the pond's edges.

conclusion

It is easy to see how important alligators are to the Everglades. The lives of so many other animals, as well as plants, depend on the water in the holes the alligators make. Thanks to the alligators, many different types of wildlife continue to live in the Everglades.

Writing the Introduction

The introduction to an essay should tell the main idea, or **thesis.** It should also grab the reader's attention and make him or her want to read on. Imagine that you are writing for a school assignment or a test. The directions for the writing assignment are called the **writing prompt.** Begin by coming up with a one-sentence answer to the writing prompt. This sentence will be your **thesis statement.**

The essay about alligator holes was a response to the following writing prompt based on an article about how alligators affect their surroundings:

WRITING PROMPT/TEST QUESTION:
Where do the alligators described in the article live and how do they change their environment? Do they help or hurt the environment?

In your response, be sure to

• identify where the alligators live,

• describe how they change their environment, and

• tell whether they help or hurt their environment.

Jenna, the student writer, came up with a one-sentence answer to this writing prompt. This sentence is the thesis statement of her essay:

"By making sure that there is a source of water throughout the dry season, alligators help many other animals and plants to survive."

Her thesis statement appears at the end of her introduction (the first paragraph of her essay).

Introduction, Body, and Conclusion

The thesis statement often comes at the end of the introduction. However, it can appear anywhere in the introductory paragraph. In many essays, the **lead,** or beginning, of the introduction comes before the thesis statement. The lead should grab the reader's attention. The lead in an introduction is usually one or two sentences, but it can be several sentences long. Think about the kind of writing you are going to do. Then think about who will be reading it. Choose the type of lead that will be the best way to get your readers interested in your topic. (When you are writing for the ELA exam, you will not have much room for a lead.)

When you have thought of an interesting way to begin your essay, write the opening or lead. Then make sure that you state your main idea clearly in your thesis statement. Remember that this is a one-sentence response (answer) to the writing prompt.

Choose a Lead for Your Introduction

- Ask a question.
- Give a quotation.
- Tell a very brief story.
- Give an interesting fact or observation.

Here is the introduction to Jenna's essay about alligator holes. As you read it again, ask yourself these questions: How did she lead into the essay? What did she do to grab the reader's attention? What is the main idea in her thesis statement? Is her thesis statement a brief answer to the prompt on page 231?

Introduction to Jenna's Essay

lead — Did you know that people are not the only creatures who go swimming to cool off on hot days? Alligators, like other reptiles, need a place to stay cool when the weather is hot. The alligators that live in the Florida Everglades survive the dry season by digging swimming holes. The alligators are not the only ones to use the holes. **thesis statement** — By making sure that there is a source of water throughout the dry season, alligators in the Everglades help many other animals and plants to survive.

Writing a Lead

Jenna began her introduction by talking about going swimming on a hot day. This is a good "grabber" sentence because many people enjoy swimming. They can understand what she is talking about. Next, she makes a connection between people and alligators by pointing out that alligators also go swimming to cool off. She provides some background information about alligators. She makes sure that readers know that alligators are reptiles and that they need a place to stay cool when it's hot.

Writing a Thesis Statement

Jenna ends the introduction with her thesis statement: *By making sure that there is a source of water throughout the dry season, alligators help many other animals and plants in their environment to survive.*

Notice that this thesis statement is a one-sentence answer to the prompt. In this sentence, Jenna has identified where the alligator lives (in the *Everglades*). She has pointed out what the alligator does to its environment. (*It makes sure there is a source of water throughout the dry season.*) She has also told whether this is helpful or harmful to the environment. (*This helps other animals and plants to survive.*) Now, in the body of her essay, she just needs to give details about how the alligator digs a swimming hole. She also needs to explain how this helps other animals.

Introduction, Body, and Conclusion

Writing the Body of the Essay

When you write an essay, you should include at least one body paragraph. Each body paragraph should discuss a main idea that supports the main point you made in your thesis statement.

Writing Topic Sentences for Paragraphs

The main idea of each paragraph should be expressed in the **topic sentence.** The topic sentence usually appears at the beginning of the paragraph. The topic sentence should be followed by details that support it. If you are asked to write about something you have read, make sure that your body paragraphs include specific details and examples from the reading to support your main idea.

Making an Outline

Here is the rough outline for the three body paragraphs in Jenna's essay on alligator holes:

Rough Outline for Body of Jenna's Essay

Topic Sentence: The Everglades is sometimes called a "river of grass."
—During wet season, grassy marshes are flooded w/water
—At end of wet season, water dries up
—Alligator pushes plants & dirt aside to create a hole
—Hole stays wet, collects water → forms little pond
—Alligator stays wet & cool

Topic Sentence: Other animals, such as fish, frogs, birds, and turtles, visit the alligator's new pond.
—Alligator has food (other animals that come for a drink)
—Other animals also have food & water
—Some animals lay eggs in pond or around edges

Topic Sentence: Plants benefit from the alligator hole, too.
—Some (water lilies) grow on water that collects in gator hole
—Others (water plants) grow at the edge
—Others (ferns, willow trees) grow in mounds of dirt around hole

---

As part of your prewriting (planning) process, you should create a rough outline for your essay. A rough outline will help you to organize your details. Then you can simply plug ideas from your outline into sentences as you write one or more body paragraphs to explain your thesis, or main idea.

Here are the body paragraphs that Jenna created from her rough outline. Notice how she turned details from her outline into complete sentences.

Body Paragraphs of Jenna's Essay

The Everglades is sometimes called a "river of grass." During the wet season, the grassy marshes are flooded with water. When the rainy season ends in October, the wet grasslands start to dry up. Then the alligator goes to work. Using its powerful legs, it pushes aside plants and dirt to make a hole in the ground. This 'gator hole becomes a little pond that holds water longer than the dry ground around it. The alligator now has a place where it can stay wet and cool.

Other animals, such as fish, frogs, birds, and turtles, visit the alligator's new pond. Some come to eat snails and small creatures that live in the water. Others come for a cool drink or to lay eggs in or near the pond. Some of these visitors become the alligator's dinner. However, many other animals are able to survive the dry season because of the water the alligator has provided.

Plants benefit from the alligator hole, too. Lily pads float on top. Water plants grow near the edges of the hole. A little farther away, ferns, willow trees and other plants that like to have "wet feet" grow in the mounds of dirt around the pond's edges.

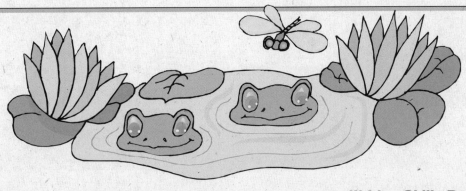

Introduction, Body, and Conclusion

Writing the Conclusion

The **conclusion** of your essay is the final part. It will usually be a single paragraph. It should sum up the ideas that you have presented in your essay using different words.

Now read the conclusion to Jenna's essay below. As you read the conclusion again, ask yourself these questions: Does the paragraph sum up the rest of the essay? What main ideas from the rest of the essay are restated in the last paragraph? Do they help Jenna make her point?

Conclusion to Jenna's Essay

It is easy to see how important alligators are to the Everglades. The lives of so many other animals, as well as plants, depend on the water in the holes the alligators make. Thanks to the alligators, many different types of wildlife continue to live in the Everglades.

Your Turn

Exercise A *Answer these questions about Jenna's essay on alligator holes. Remember to use complete sentences in your answers.*

1. What is the thesis statement of the essay? Where does this thesis statement appear in the essay?

   _____

   _____

2. How does Jenna grab her readers' attention in the first paragraph?

   _____

   _____

3. What are the topic sentences of the body paragraphs? Where do these sentences appear in the paragraphs?

   _____

   _____

   _____

4. What specific details does Jenna include in the body paragraphs to support each topic sentence? Where do you think she found these details?

   _____

   _____

   _____

5. Which words or phrases does Jenna use in her essay to help connect ideas?

   _____

   _____

More ▶

6. Which sentence in the conclusion repeats the overall idea of the thesis statement (Jenna's main point) using different words?

_____

Exercise B *For the ELA examination, you will have to write extended responses based on a listening passage and a pair of reading passages. The directions will tell you what kind of writing you need to do. Like any other essay, your extended responses should have an introduction, a body, and a conclusion, although your conclusion may be just one sentence. Follow these steps to write an extended response:*

STEP 1   Reread the story and the poem at the beginning of Unit 3 (pages 110–112).

STEP 2   Analyze this prompt:

The story "Mr. Handyman" and the poem "Thanks to Dad" share a similar lesson, or theme. What is the theme of the story, and what is the theme of the poem? How are the themes similar? Use details from **both** the story and the poem to explain your answer.

In your answer, be sure to

- explain the theme of the story
- explain the theme of the poem
- tell how the themes are similar
- include details from **both** the story and the poem

PURPOSE: _____

_____

DETAILS TO INCLUDE: _____

STEP 3   Write a one-sentence answer to the prompt that can serve as the thesis statement for your response.

THESIS STATEMENT: _____

_____

STEP **4**   Choose a graphic organizer and, on your own paper, gather details from both selections to use in your response.

STEP **5**   Draft your response on the lines below.

_____

_____

_____

_____

_____

_____

_____

_____

_____

_____

_____

_____

_____

_____

More ▶

Your Turn

_____

_____

_____

_____

_____

_____

_____

_____

_____

_____

_____

_____

_____

_____

_____

_____

_____

STEP 6   Reread your response, then revise and proofread it using the Revision
Checklist on page 196 and the Proofreading Checklist on page 199.
Use the Revision and Proofreading Symbols on page 200 to make
your edits.

Return to the exercises
at the beginning of the
unit. Check your work
and fix it if necessary.
Give the exercises to
your teacher for grading.

Posttest
English Language Arts

Session 1: Reading

In this part of the test, you are going to do some reading. Then you will answer questions about what you have read.

Session 1: Reading

Directions *Read this article about a dinosaur expert. Then answer questions 1 through 5.*

Jurassic Genius
by Manuel Romero

When Jack Horner was a young boy in Montana, he just couldn't understand the words in his books. Sometimes he wrote his letters backwards. His mind seemed to work differently.

Jack did not do well in school, but he was very good at something else. He loved dinosaurs, and he knew a lot about them. He spent his free time searching for fossils in the hills of Montana. Fossils are bones and other remains of ancient animals and plants found in old rocks. Jack found his first dinosaur fossil when he was only eight years old.

Jack tried going to college, but he never finished. He went to work for his family's business instead. He spent his weekends looking for fossils. In 1975, he got a job in New Jersey, but every summer he returned to Montana to look for more fossils.

In 1978, someone in Montana showed Jack Horner and his friend Bob Makela some little fossil bones. Horner saw right away that these were the bones of baby dinosaurs! Horner and Makela kept

digging where the bones had been uncovered. Before long, they made an amazing discovery. They came upon the fossilized remains of North America's first known dinosaur nest. The nest they found was more than sixty million years old! In the nest, buried in the rock, were fossils of dinosaur eggshells.

Ever since then, Jack Horner has continued his search for fossils of dinosaur nests and eggs. It is hard work. Horner often has to crawl over rocks on his hands and knees in the hot sun. He uses small tools to chip away at rocks in search of little pieces of fossilized eggshells. All the hard work has been worth it. Horner has discovered the eggs and nests of two different kinds of dinosaur.

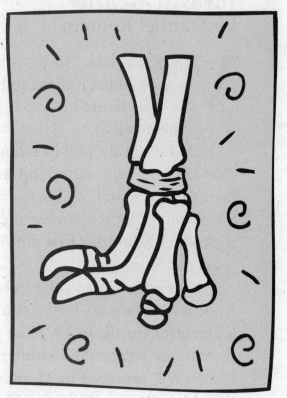

Jack Horner has become an expert on dinosaurs. Even though he had problems in school when he was young, he now teaches at a college. When people want to know about dinosaurs, they often come to him. He helped the people who made the movie *Jurassic Park* and its sequel, *The Lost World*. He showed them how to make the dinosaurs look and act real. Some people say that the character of one of the scientists in the movies is based on Jack Horner. When people in Japan wanted to make a dinosaur park with life-sized dinosaur robots, they asked Jack Horner to help them.

Recently, Jack Horner earned a MacArthur Foundation award for his discoveries about dinosaurs. Who would have guessed that the little boy who got bad grades in school would one day be recognized as a genius? Jack Horner's story proves that sometimes even very smart people have a hard time in school. Other brilliant people who had trouble in school when they were young include Albert Einstein and James Watson, two of the greatest scientists of the twentieth century. Jack Horner is in excellent company. ○

1. What amazing discovery did Jack Horner and his friend Bob make?
   - Ⓐ They found the remains of dinosaur-sized robots.
   - Ⓑ They found the bones of some ancient baby birds in a nest.
   - Ⓒ They found the remains of the first known dinosaur nest in North America.
   - Ⓓ They found the script for the movie *Jurassic Park*.

2. According to this passage, why did Jack have trouble in school?
   - Ⓐ The teachers did not like dinosaurs.
   - Ⓑ His mind worked differently.
   - Ⓒ The other children were smarter than he was.
   - Ⓓ He was always playing tricks on the teachers.

3. Read this sentence from the article:

   [Jack Horner] helped the people who made the movie *Jurassic Park* and its sequel, *The Lost World*.

   What is a *sequel*?
   - Ⓐ something that comes before something else
   - Ⓑ something that follows or continues the same story
   - Ⓒ something that makes something else happen
   - Ⓓ something that is equal to, or the same as, something else

4. Why did Jack earn an award from the MacArthur Foundation?
   - Ⓐ He won the award for his work with fossilized insects.
   - Ⓑ He won the award for his work with dinosaur fossils.
   - Ⓒ He won the award for his work with Japanese cars.
   - Ⓓ He won the award for his work on the movie *Jurassic Park*.

5. Why did the author tell us about Einstein and Watson?
   - Ⓐ to make the point that all scientists like dinosaurs and fossils
   - Ⓑ to make the point that even geniuses can have trouble in school
   - Ⓒ to make the point that Jack and Bob were geniuses, too
   - Ⓓ to make the point that all scientists like to go to the movies

Directions *Read this article about honeybees. Then answer questions 6 through 11.*

Honeybees in the Army
by Kai Funaki

Have you ever wondered how honeybees communicate? For many years, scientists have studied this amazing process. As far as bee experts can tell, it works something like this: A honeybee finds a good source of nectar, a sugary food found in flowers. The bee collects some of the nectar and then flies back to the hive. At the hive, the bee passes out samples of the nectar to other bees. In order to tell the other bees where the nectar came from, the honeybee does a dance that shows the other bees where to go.

Honeybees do many dances. Each one gives different information. One is called the round dance. It is done to show that food is close to the hive. The round dance does not tell where nectar is located, but the bee spreads the smell of the nectar as it dances. Since the food is fairly close to the hive, the other bees can find it using their keen sense of smell.

Another bee dance is the waggle dance, which means that a food source is more than thirty-five yards (thirty-two meters) from the hive. The waggle dance actually tells the direction and distance to a source of food. One move the bee makes in this dance is a straight crawl. This move tells the direction to the food, in relation to the sun's position in the sky. The length of the straight crawl may tell the other bees the distance to the food source. Scientists also think that bee dancers describe distances by how long they buzz. Bees usually look for food within three miles (about five kilometers) of the hive. Sometimes, though, bees travel seven miles (about twelve kilometers) or more while looking for food.

Scientists have studied bees to collect information about the places where they fly. Pollen is not the only thing a bee might pick up if it lands on something. Because things that bees touch often stick to their bodies, scientists have used bees to find pollutants. The Environmental Protection Agency (EPA) has even approved bees as data collectors. Sometimes a honeybee can take a better survey than a person can.

Scientists have found another possible use for bees. Bee experts think that bees might be able to find landmines. Landmines are bombs that are buried or half-buried underground. The mines explode when something walks or drives on the ground above them. In some places, people have buried lots of landmines during wars. The landmines can hurt many people, long after the fighting is over. If landmines are not cleared, the land is too dangerous for farming or for building homes or businesses.

Bees are very easy to train. Sometimes it only takes a few hours. Researchers in several places are training bees to identify TNT. TNT is the main explosive in most landmines. Traces of TNT leak into the ground or water near landmines. Scientists train the bees to find TNT by mixing small amounts of TNT and sugar. The bees go to the sugar. Very soon, they begin to associate TNT with sugar. This means that if they smell TNT, they will think it is a source of food. Because bees have such a strong sense of smell, they can find tiny amounts of TNT that have spread out from the landmines into nearby plants and soil.

As you might guess, if bees think that TNT is a source of food, then when they find some, they will return to the hive to tell other bees where it is. Knowing this, scientists can examine bees that return to the hive and check whether the bees are carrying small amounts of TNT. Scientists also put tiny radio devices on the bees. In this way, people can track where the TNT-seeking bees are going. If people suspect that there are landmines in an area, bees could be used to find out exactly where the landmines are. Once people know where the landmines are, they can be exploded without harming anyone.

There are beekeepers or wild bees in almost every part of the world. This means that scientists could go to an area with landmines and quickly train local bees to find the explosives, instead of using bomb-sniffing dogs, hired labor, or expensive robots. Honeybees already make the world a sweeter place. Soon they could make it a safer one, too. ○

The chart below describes some common bee movements and what they "tell" other bees in the hive. Use the chart and information from the article to answer questions 6 and 7.

Bee's Movement	Tells Other Bees
round dance	①
waggle dance	②
straight crawl	direction to food source

6. Which information belongs in the space marked ①?
   Ⓐ there is food close to the hive
   Ⓑ there is no food to be found
   Ⓒ there is food more than thirty-five yards from the hive
   Ⓓ there is food more than three miles from the hive

7. Which information belongs in the space marked ②?
   Ⓐ there is food close to the hive
   Ⓑ there is no food to be found
   Ⓒ there is food more than thirty-five yards from the hive
   Ⓓ there is food more than three miles from the hive

8. Read this sentence from the article:

   Since the food is fairly close to the hive, the other bees can find it using their keen sense of smell.

   What does *keen* mean?
   Ⓐ bad or useless
   Ⓑ smart or intelligent
   Ⓒ sharp or sensitive
   Ⓓ fast or speedy

9. What probably happens after a bee "tells" other bees where to find food?

    Ⓐ The bees stay in the hive.

    Ⓑ The other bees fly around the hive.

    Ⓒ The other bees fly to the food source.

    Ⓓ The other bees dance for a few minutes.

10. Why are bees useful for telling scientists about pollution in an area?

    Ⓐ because the things that bees touch often stick to their bodies

    Ⓑ because bees die when pollutants touch their wings

    Ⓒ because bees do a special dance after they swallow TNT

    Ⓓ because bees do a special dance after they breathe in smog

11. The author of the article would most likely agree with which of the following statements?

    Ⓐ It is hard to train honeybees because they are so small.

    Ⓑ Landmines are no longer a danger in most of the world.

    Ⓒ Bees could help humans in many new ways.

    Ⓓ Honeybees are the only creatures that dance.

GO ON

Directions Read this article about a famous cartoonist (an artist who draws comic strips). Then answer questions 12 through 17.

Making Peanuts
by Cynthia Nye

Arrrrrrgh!

Does this scene sound familiar? A boy runs toward a girl holding a football for him to kick. Just as he reaches her, she pulls the ball away. His leg swings wildly, and he falls backward onto the ground. "Some people never learn," the girl says, and she walks away.

This is one of the most famous Charlie Brown moments. Charlie Brown is the thoughtful main character of the comic strip "Peanuts," drawn by the great cartoonist Charles M. Schulz. What a lot of people don't know is that Charles Schulz created "Peanuts" from his own life experiences. Like Charlie Brown, young Schulz was a misfit. He was a skinny kid with big ears, who was smarter and more serious than most of the other kids around him. Schulz was so smart that he skipped two grades, but he was lonely and unhappy in school. He was the youngest and smallest boy in his class, and he had very few friends. He often felt that no one noticed his talents.

One thing Schulz knew he could do well was to draw. He loved reading comic books, and he decided at an early age to become a cartoonist. He sometimes used his notebooks for drawing instead of schoolwork. One hint of his future success came at age 15, when Schulz's drawing of his dog Spike was published in the "Ripley's Believe It or Not"™ comic strip in the *New York Globe*. Spike gave Schulz the idea for Snoopy, Charlie Brown's dog.

In high school, Schulz took a cartooning class by mail. Eventually, he became a teacher for the course. He knew that he had talent, but none of his teachers or classmates at his high school seemed to notice. He was deeply hurt when the editors of his high-school yearbook rejected a collection of his drawings. He resented this until his dying day.

After high school, Schulz went to Europe to fight in World War II. When he returned, he began drawing a comic strip that he called "Li'l Folks." Several publishers rejected Schulz's comic strip. One company finally agreed to publish "Li'l Folks," but they would not pay Schulz. Then, in 1950, a company called United Feature Syndicate began running his comic strip in several newspapers. The company renamed the strip "Peanuts." Schulz hated the name, but he had to go along with it.

It took about a year before "Peanuts" really caught on. Eventually, it became the most popular comic strip on the planet. It has been translated into more than twenty languages and printed all over the world. The astronauts of the *Apollo 10* mission even took "Peanuts" to the moon: They nicknamed their spaceship Charlie Brown and their landing module Snoopy! A play called *You're a Good Man, Charlie Brown,* which was based on the comic strip, is one of the most-performed plays in American theater. Schulz also wrote "Peanuts" books and television specials that are still popular today.

Perhaps one of the reasons that "Peanuts" became so popular is that, when it first came out, it was so different from other comic strips. It was the first comic strip in which all the human characters were realistic.

There are no superheroes in the "Peanuts" gang. They live in an ordinary world and have problems that real people face. Both children and adults can laugh at a "Peanuts" cartoon and understand the message behind it.

Although "Peanuts" made Schulz famous and wealthy, he always thought of himself as an ordinary man—a person much like Charlie Brown. He never let his success go to his head. After he became famous, Schulz said,

"I don't think I'm a true artist. I would love to be Andrew Wyeth or Picasso…But I can draw pretty well, and I can write pretty well. I think I'm doing the best with whatever abilities I have been given. What more can one ask?" Charles Schulz drew "Peanuts" for almost fifty years, until his eyesight failed and his hands shook with illness. Finally, he decided it was time to retire. He sent in his last strip. Then, on February 12, 2000, at the age of 77, Schulz died. The next day, his final Sunday "Peanuts" comic strip appeared in newspapers. With it was his message of farewell. The message was a simple thank you to his editors and his many fans. Charles Schulz has said goodbye, but he lives on in "Peanuts." ○

12. What is this article MOSTLY about?

Ⓐ how to create a best-selling comic strip

Ⓑ how to think of interesting cartoon characters

Ⓒ Charles Schulz, one of the most famous cartoonists in the world

Ⓓ Charles Schulz's experiences as a soldier in World War II

13. What detail does the author include to show readers that Schulz was a very bright child?

Ⓐ Schulz drew in his notebooks instead of doing schoolwork.

Ⓑ One of Schulz's drawings was published in "Ripley's Believe It or Not."™

Ⓒ Schulz could play the piano at the age of four.

Ⓓ Schulz skipped two grade levels in school.

14. Which of the following happened FIRST?

Ⓐ Schulz taught a cartooning class by mail.

Ⓑ United Feature Syndicate began running Schulz's comic strip in newspapers.

Ⓒ Schulz's drawing of his dog was published in "Ripley's Believe It or Not."™

Ⓓ A play was written based on Schulz's comic strip "Peanuts."

15. Read these sentences from the article:

He was deeply hurt when the editors of his high-school yearbook rejected a collection of his drawings. He resented this until his dying day.

What does *resent* mean in this sentence?

Ⓐ to send something over and over again

Ⓑ to appreciate something very much

Ⓒ to feel angry about something that seems mean or unfair

Ⓓ to feel happy about something that seems mean or unfair

16. How was Schulz's comic strip DIFFERENT from other comic strips that were published when it first came out?
    Ⓐ It was printed in color.
    Ⓑ The human characters were all realistic.
    Ⓒ It was written mainly for adults.
    Ⓓ The characters were all superheroes.

17. What would be another good title for this reading passage?
    Ⓐ "Why Charles Schulz Liked to Draw"
    Ⓑ "Why Snoopy Liked Charlie Brown"
    Ⓒ "Why Schulz Named His Comic Strip 'Peanuts'"
    Ⓓ "Charles Schulz: The Real Charlie Brown"

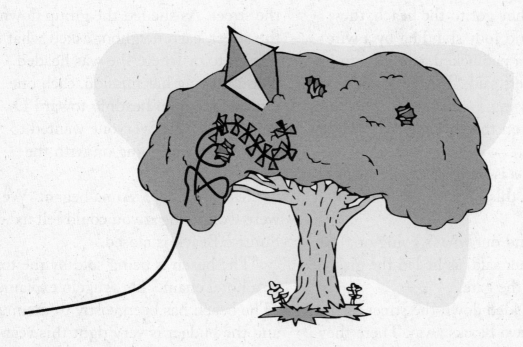

GO ON

Directions *Read this story. Then answer questions 18 through 22.*

Saving Sunrise
by Lee Donatello

Early Saturday morning, Mary and her family headed toward Sunrise Beach. Mary was excited because Jody and Ellie, her favorite cousins, were joining them at the beach. They could get a nice picnic area near the volleyball courts if they arrived early. By noon, the beach would be crowded.

"I can't wait to play beach volleyball with Ellie and Jody again," said Mary.

"Yeah, you all make a great team," her father replied.

When they got to the beach, they saw Ellie and Jody standing by a wire fence with a padlocked gate. A sign in big red letters said, "Private Property. No Trespassing."

"Are we on the wrong beach?" Ellie asked.

"No. This is Sunrise Beach. I don't understand this," Mary said with a knit brow.

"Let's find out what's going on," Mary's father said, as he led the girls away from the gate.

They headed down the street to the bike shop two blocks away. There they found Anna Lopez, the owner of the store, peering at a catalog.

"Excuse me," Mary said. "Do you know why the beach is closed?"

Anna looked up. "I've been wondering that myself," she said in a deep, scratchy voice. "They just put that sign up last week. Dr. Angelo would know. He's a member of the town council. Let's go see him. His office is just down the street."

Anna seemed to know everyone on the street. As she led the group down the street, each neighbor asked what she was up to or where she was headed. Upon hearing her mission, each one joined the group heading toward Dr. Angelo's office. Everyone wanted to know what was going on with the beach.

"Mornin', Doc," Anna began. "We were wondering if you could tell us why Sunrise Beach is closed."

"The beach is being sold by the town to a hotel chain," Dr. Angelo explained. "The beach has been costly to maintain, and the budget is very tight this year. The town simply cannot afford to keep the beach as a public beach anymore."

The crowd buzzed with concern.

"You said the beach is *being* sold. Does that mean they haven't sold it yet?" Mary asked.

"Well," said Dr. Angelo, "the council members are supposed to vote next Monday on whether to approve the sale."

"Is there something that we can do to stop it?" Mary asked eagerly.

"Maybe, the doctor replied. "Maintaining that beach is expensive. First you would have to come up with some way that the town could cover the costs. Then you would have to get enough people to support the idea. If you could do that, you might have a chance of blocking the sale."

The girls were quiet as they followed Mary's father back to the house.

At Mary's house, the girls hatched a plan. First, they told Mary's brother, Arthur, about the beach. He picked up the phone and called all his friends. He asked them to write letters to the town council, asking them to vote against the sale of the beach. Then he started working on the computer. Meanwhile, Mary got out some markers, Jody and Ellie found some poster board, and the girls went to work.

The next morning, dozens of letters were on their way to all the members of the town council. The local newspapers also received a few letters. The *Daily Times* printed a letter from Arthur on its editorial page. Part of it read, "Sunrise Beach should not be sold. Our families need it. The beach can be maintained without costing the town a penny."

Posters hung on every street corner pleading, "Save Sunrise!" On street corners throughout the town, volunteers asked for signatures on a petition.

At last, the day of the council meeting came. Mary, Ellie, Jody, and many other volunteers went to Town Hall early and were waiting on the steps when Dr. Angelo arrived. Mary handed him a petition to keep the beach open to everyone. It stressed that Sunrise Beach was vital to the community. It also suggested that local businesses be allowed to build a boardwalk on the beach with stores along it. The stores would take responsibility for maintaining the beach. The petition even listed a group of business owners who would be interested in participating. More than two hundred people in town had signed the petition. Dr. Angelo accepted the petition and promised to present it to the council members.

"I will contact you tomorrow to let you know the final decision," the doctor said to Mary.

"Thank you, but I would rather wait here until you come out." Mary replied politely. Others murmured and nodded in agreement.

Dr. Angelo disappeared through the huge, polished doors of the town hall. For three hours, Mary and the others sat on the steps, waiting. Finally, Dr. Angelo reappeared. Without a word, he raised one hand and stuck his thumb up. ○

GO ON ⇨

18. What is Mary's BIGGEST problem in this story?
    Ⓐ She must figure out how to get along with her cousins.
    Ⓑ She must figure out a way to win the volleyball tournament.
    Ⓒ She must figure out a way to save the town beach.
    Ⓓ She must figure out a way to clean up the town beach.

19. What does Mary expect to happen when she arrives at Sunrise Beach?
    Ⓐ She expects the beach to be very crowded.
    Ⓑ She expects to play volleyball with her cousins.
    Ⓒ She expects to eat lunch on the boardwalk.
    Ⓓ She expects to see many of her friends.

20. Read this sentence from the story:

    [The petition] stressed that the beach was vital to the community.

    What does the word *vital* mean?
    Ⓐ not important   Ⓑ annoying   Ⓒ beautiful   Ⓓ very important

21. How does Mary's brother help her save the beach?
    Ⓐ He asks his friends to write letters to council members, and he writes a letter to the newspaper.
    Ⓑ He meets with the council and then writes the petition and presents it to the council.
    Ⓒ He helps Mary and her friends make posters and goes all over town hanging them up.
    Ⓓ He invites all of his friends over and plans a fundraiser to raise money for the beach.

22. What was the author's purpose in writing this story?
    Ⓐ to show that young people can make a difference when they get together and take action
    Ⓑ to show that working together means listening to everyone's ideas and opinions
    Ⓒ to show that communities are better off when they keep their beaches instead of selling them
    Ⓓ to show that adults do not usually listen to young people or take their advice

Directions *Read this article about food labels. Then answer questions 23 through 28.*

You Are What You Eat
by Tory Lucre

Have you ever found yourself sitting at the breakfast table barely awake, staring at the label on the side of the cereal box and wondering what all those words and numbers mean? If you've never looked at the labels on the foods you eat, then you should. After all, you are what you eat, as the old saying goes. Paying attention to the labels on foods is one way to make sure you are eating a balanced diet, which is a key to good health.

Nutrition Facts

Serving Size 1/2 cup (114g)
Servings Per Container 3

Amount per serving

Calories 100   Fat Cal. 27

Let's look at a food label and what its parts mean: "Serving size" and "Servings per container" are important items that are sometimes overlooked. The heading "Amount per serving" shows that the rest of the information in the label is based on the serving size. However, people often eat more than one serving at a time. This food product has 100 calories *in each 1/2 cup serving,* and there are three servings in the package. If you ate the whole package, then you would be consuming 300 calories (100 calories × 3 servings). It is important to note the serving size as well as how many servings there are in the package.

A **calorie** is a measurement of the amount of energy your body gets from a food source. Your body needs calories to operate, much as a car needs gas to run. But if you eat more calories than your body uses up each day, you will gain weight. Most people should eat between 1,300 and 2,000 calories a day.

Fat calories are the number of the calories in a serving that come from fat. The more fat calories a food has, the more likely you are to gain weight from eating that food. Generally, you should choose foods in which less than 30 percent (%) of the calories come from fat.

Under the heading "% of Daily Value" you will see percentages, or numbers based on the total amount of each nutrient that you should eat in a day. For example, health experts say that most people should eat no more than 65 grams of fat per day. This food product has 3 grams of fat per serving. Three grams (out of 65) is about 5 percent of the total grams of fat that you should eat in a day.

Saturated fat is a type of fat that comes mainly from meat and dairy products. It is worse for you than other types of fat. No more than 20 of your 65 daily grams of fat should come from saturated fat.

Cholesterol is a fat-like substance found in your blood. Your body needs some cholesterol to stay healthy, but too much cholesterol can clog your blood vessels. This can lead to serious health problems. You should try to eat no more than 300 milligrams (mg) of cholesterol each day.

Salty foods are high in **sodium.** Eating too much sodium can lead to health problems such as high blood pressure.

Nutrition Facts

<u>Serving Size</u> 1/2 cup (114g)
<u>Servings Per Container</u> 3

<u>Amount per serving</u>

<u>Calories</u> 100	Fat Cal. 27

% Daily Value*

<u>Total Fat</u> 3g	5%
Saturated Fat 0g	0%
<u>Cholesterol</u> 0mg	0%
<u>Sodium</u> 300mg	13%
<u>Total Carbohydrate</u> 13mg	4%
Dietary Fiber 3g	12%
Sugars 3g	12%
<u>Protein</u> 3g	
<u>Vitamin A</u> 80%	<u>Vitamin C</u> 60%
<u>Calcium</u> 4%	<u>Iron</u> 4%

*Percent Daily Values are based on a 2,000 calorie diet. Your daily values may be higher or lower depending on your calorie needs.

Carbohydrates are found in such foods as milk, fruits, some vegetables, breads, cereals, and grains. Carbohydrates should make up the majority of your diet. Carbohydrates that contain fiber are particularly good for you. Fiber is a material that cannot be digested, so it helps to move food through your system.

Protein is found in meats, nuts, beans, and dairy products. Protein is very important for a healthy body, but many Americans eat more protein than they really need. About 10 percent of your total daily calories should come from protein.

Vitamins and **minerals,** such as calcium and iron, are also necessary for your body to function properly. Vitamins and minerals are added to many food products today. Some of the best sources of vitamins and minerals, however, are fruits and vegetables—foods that don't come with labels.

Try to make a habit of looking at the labels on foods you eat. In general, you should go for foods that are low in fat, cholesterol, and calories, yet high in fiber. Eating a well-balanced diet and getting plenty of exercise are the best things you can do to stay healthy. And as the great philosopher Ralph Waldo Emerson said, "The first wealth is health." ○

GO ON

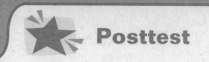

23. Why did the author write this article?

    Ⓐ to persuade young people to get outside and get more exercise

    Ⓑ to explain the different types of cholesterol found in the body

    Ⓒ to entertain readers with stories about errors on food labels

    Ⓓ to explain food labels and to encourage healthy eating habits

24. If you were to eat the entire package of food described by the label, what percentage of your recommended daily fat would you have eaten?

    Ⓐ about 5%

    Ⓑ about 65%

    Ⓒ about 25%

    Ⓓ about 15%

25. According to the article, which of the following should make up the majority of your calories each day?

    Ⓐ fat

    Ⓑ carbohydrates

    Ⓒ sodium

    Ⓓ protein

26. Read this sentence from the article:

    If you ate the whole package, then you would be consuming 300 calories.

    What does the word *consuming* mean?

    Ⓐ buying

    Ⓑ selling

    Ⓒ eating

    Ⓓ burning off

27. What is a calorie?

    Ⓐ a measurement of the amount of energy provided by a food source

    Ⓑ a type of sugar found in some foods that are high in fat

    Ⓒ a type of fat found in the bloodstream that can cause clogging

    Ⓓ a measurement of the amount of fat that is found in a food source

28. According to the article, you should do the following things to stay healthy:

1. Look at the labels on the foods you eat.
2.
3. Get plenty of exercise.

Choose the answer that best completes the chart above.

Ⓐ Eat foods that are high in protein, cholesterol, and minerals, yet low in fat.

Ⓑ Eat fewer than 1300 calories per day.

Ⓒ Eat foods that are low in fat, cholesterol, and calories, yet high in fiber.

Ⓓ Avoid eating foods that do not come with labels.

 **Stop! End of Session 1**

The rest of the test asks you to write about what you have listened to or read. Your writing will NOT be scored on your personal opinions. It WILL be scored on:

- how clearly you organize and express your ideas
- how accurately and completely you answer the questions
- how well you support your ideas with examples
- how interesting and enjoyable your writing is
- how correctly you use grammar, spelling, punctuation, and paragraphs

 Whenever you see this symbol, be sure to plan and check your writing.

Session 2: Listening and Writing

Directions In this part of the test, you are going to listen to a story called "Tina's Talent," by Anita Cadet. Then you will answer some questions about the story.

You will listen to the story twice. The first time you hear the story, listen carefully but do not take notes. As you listen to the story the second time, you may want to take notes. Use the space below for your notes. You may use these notes to answer the questions that follow. Your notes on this page will NOT count toward your final score.

Notes

Do NOT turn this page until you are told to do so.

Note to Teachers: This listening selection appears on pages 35–36 in the Teacher's Guide for AIM Higher! New York ELA Review.

29. How do Tina's feelings about being on the soccer team change from the beginning of the story to the end? Why do her feelings change?

_____

_____

_____

_____

_____

_____

30. In the box below, list three things that Tina does to help make the car wash a success.

Tina helps to make the car wash a success by...
1. _____ _____
2. _____ _____
3. _____ _____

Planning Page

You may PLAN your writing for question 31 here if you wish, but do NOT write your final answer on this page. Your writing on this Planning Page will NOT count toward your final score. Write your final answer beginning on the next page.

31. What talent does Tina discover that she has? How is her talent useful to the soccer team? Do you think that Tina should stay on the soccer team, or should she try some other activities?

In your answer, be sure to

- describe Tina's talent

- tell how her talent is useful to the soccer team

- explain why Tina should stay on the soccer team, or why she should try other activities

- use details from the story to explain your answer

 Check your writing for correct spelling, grammar, and punctuation.

_____

_____

_____

_____

_____

_____

_____

_____

_____

_____

_____

_____

_____

_____

_____

_____

_____

_____

_____

_____

_____

_____

_____

_____

_____

_____

 Stop! End of Session 2

Posttest

Session 3: Reading and Writing

Directions In this part of the test, you are going to read an article called "The Man Who Wouldn't Quit" and a poem called "Don't Quit." Then answer questions 32 through 35 and write about what you have read. You may look back at the article and the poem as often as you like.

The Man Who Wouldn't Quit
by Sterling Moore

It takes great courage and determination to make it to the Olympics. Athletes often spend their lives training with the hope of winning a single event. So, you can imagine the pressure that Olympic athletes must feel. That pressure is even greater when the athlete is expected to win. Dan Jansen was an American speed skater, a champion who set world records. Everyone expected him to win, but he had to compete in four Olympics before he finally won a gold medal.

Dan Jansen grew up in a suburb outside of Milwaukee, Wisconsin. He was the youngest of nine children. He spent much of his early childhood watching his older brothers and sisters race in speed-skating competitions. Jansen's older sister, Jane, was the one who taught him how to skate. He was a natural, and it was not long before he began winning races. His best event was the 500-meter race. As a sophomore in high school, Dan Jansen set the junior world record in this event at an international competition.

Just two years later, in 1984, Jansen competed in his first Olympics. He was only eighteen years old, and no one expected him to win. He was thrilled when he came in fourth in the 500-meter race. At home, however, the reporters treated his fourth-place finish as a major defeat because he did not win a medal. Nevertheless, Jansen continued to work hard to improve his skating. By 1986, he was number one in the world in both the 500- and 1000-meter events.

The next year, Jansen faced some setbacks. He came down with an illness called mononucleosis, which left him with little strength to train and compete. Around the same time, he found out that his sister Jane had a type of cancer called leukemia. In spite of these problems, Jansen qualified for the 1988 Winter Olympics in Canada. This time, the pressure was greater. He was considered the favorite to win the 500-meter event.

GO ON

On the morning of the event, he received a phone call from Jane. Then, just hours before his race, Jansen found out that his sister had passed away. He thought about dropping out of the event, but his mother encouraged him to race. Understandably, he was too upset to focus on skating. First he made a false start, and then, ten seconds into the race, he slipped and fell. He was disqualified. Jansen did the same thing in the 1000-meter event four days later. Far from winning a medal, he did not even finish either of his races.

Jansen did not let these events or his sister's death stop him. He continued to train and became better than ever. In 1991, Jansen won the 500-meter event at the U.S. Olympic trials. A month later, he set the world record for that distance. In 1992, he entered his third Olympics. Again, he was the favorite to win the 500- and 1000-meter speed-skating events. But Jansen's hopes for a gold medal were dashed again. This time, he did not slip, but he did not skate as fast as he had been skating in the months leading up to the Olympics.

Some people blamed his disappointing performance on the skating conditions. They said that the ice was too soft because of rain and warm temperatures. Others claimed that Jansen's nerves got the better of him.

Rather than let the critics discourage him, Jansen continued training. The next year, he became the first speed skater ever to skate 500 meters in less than 36 seconds. He did this three more times before the beginning of the 1994 Winter Olympics in Lillehammer, Norway. No other skater had broken the 36-second barrier even once. Without a doubt, Jansen was the fastest speed skater in the world. Yet some critics predicted that he would choke once again. He seemed to prove them right when a slight slip in the 500-meter event left him in eighth place.

Jansen entered the 1000-meter event a few days later, knowing that it was his last chance to win an Olympic medal. Later, in an interview, Jansen claimed that before this final race he had said to himself, "Just don't expect things anymore, and just go out and see what happens." What happened was that Jansen flew off the starting line and skated faster than he or anyone else ever had. Finally, after ten years of Olympic competition, Jansen won his gold medal. In one of the most emotional moments in Olympic history, Jansen skated his victory lap carrying his eight-month-old daughter, Jane, named after his sister. ◎

32. The timeline below is missing two entries. Fill in the missing information in the blank boxes in the timeline.

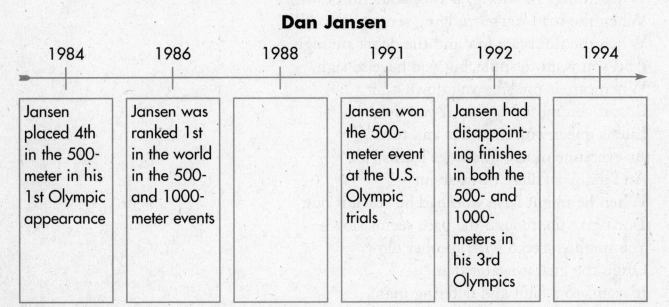

Dan Jansen

1984	1986	1988	1991	1992	1994
Jansen placed 4th in the 500-meter in his 1st Olympic appearance	Jansen was ranked 1st in the world in the 500- and 1000-meter events		Jansen won the 500-meter event at the U.S. Olympic trials	Jansen had disappointing finishes in both the 500- and 1000-meters in his 3rd Olympics	

33. The author of the article says that all Olympic athletes feel pressure, but the pressure is greatest "when the athlete is expected to win." How did high expectations from others and from himself seem to affect Dan Jansen's performance?

_____

_____

_____

_____

_____

_____

GO ON

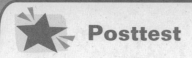
Don't Quit

When things go wrong, as they sometimes will,
When the road you're trudging seems all up hill,
When the funds are low and the debts are high,
And you want to smile, but you have to sigh,
When care is pressing you down a bit,
Rest if you must—but don't you quit!
Life is queer with its twists and turns,
As everyone of us sometimes learns,
And many a failure turns about
When he might have won had he stuck it out;
Don't give up, though the pace seems slow—
You might succeed with another blow.
Often the goal is nearer than
It seems to a faint and faltering man,
When he might have captured the victor's cup.
And he learned too late, when the night slipped down,
How close he was to the golden crown.
Success is failure turned inside out—
The silver tint of the clouds of doubt—
And you never can tell how close you are,
It may be near when it seems afar;
So stick to the fight when you're hardest hit—
It's when things seem worst that you must not quit. ○

—Unknown

34. Throughout the poem, the speaker points out that people often give up just when they are about to succeed. One example is provided on the lines below. Write two more pairs of lines from the poem in which the speaker makes this same point.

1. "Don't give up, though the pace seems slow— /

   You might succeed with another blow."

2. _____ /

   _____

3. _____ /

   _____

GO ON

Planning Page

You may PLAN your writing for question 35 here if you wish, but do NOT write your final answer on this page. Your writing on this Planning Page will NOT count toward your final score. Write your final answer beginning on the next page.

35. Did Dan Jansen seem to follow the advice given in the poem?
Explain how.

In your answer, be sure to

- tell what advice the poem gives

- explain how Dan Jansen followed this advice

- use examples from BOTH the article and the poem to support
  your answer

Check your writing for correct spelling, grammar, and punctuation.

_____

_____

_____

_____

_____

_____

_____

_____

_____

_____

GO ON

_____

_____

_____

_____

_____

_____

_____

_____

_____

_____

_____

_____

_____

_____

_____

_____

_____

Stop! End of Test

Appendix A:
Punctuation and Capitalization Handbook

1. End Marks

1.1 A declarative sentence ends with a period (.).

> The sun is a very close star.

1.2 A question ends with a question mark (?).

> How hot is the surface of the sun?

1.3 An exclamation, or strong statement, ends with an exclamation mark (!). A strong imperative statement, or command, can also end with an exclamation mark.

> Wow!

> The temperature inside the sun is 27,000,000°F!

2. Commas

2.1 Use a comma after an introductory exclamation or interjection, participial phrase, or adverbial clause. (A **clause** is a group of words that has a subject and a verb.)

AFTER INTERJECTION	Well, in only a few short months, the farm was overrun by rabbits.
AFTER PARTICIPIAL PHRASE	Hanging from a branch by one hand, the monkey chattered and hooted.
ADVERBIAL CLAUSE	After we got the puppy, life was crazy around our house for a while.

2.2 Use a comma after two or more introductory prepositional phrases if these phrases are not immediately followed by a verb.

NOT FOLLOWED BY VERB	At the end of the story, the prince decides to become a frog again.
FOLLOWED BY VERB	Through the door and into the class walked a golden retriever.

2.3 Use commas to set off an element that interrupts a sentence. Such an interrupter is known as a **parenthetical expression.**

> This rug, for example, was woven in Iran.

More ▶

2.4 Use commas to separate items in a series, including words, phrases, and clauses.

| TO SEPARATE WORDS | My favorite characters are Snoopy, Woodstock, and Linus. |
| TO SEPARATE GROUPS OF WORDS | At school we get to play music, to do art, and to act in dramas. |

Do not use commas to separate items when each is joined by a coordinating conjunction like *and, or,* or *nor.*

| USE COMMAS | We bought kibble, a leash, and a collar. |
| DO NOT USE COMMAS | We bought kibble and a leash and a collar. |

2.5 Use commas to separate two or more adjectives that describe a noun.

| USE COMMAS | These are slick, icy roads. |

2.6 Use commas to separate two independent clauses joined by *and, or, nor, for, but, so,* or *yet.* (An **independent clause** is a group of words that has a subject and verb and that can stand alone as a sentence.)

Grizzlies look cuddly, but they are very dangerous.

2.7 Use a comma to set off a direct quotation after the verb in a speaker's tag.

The astronaut said, "Fly me to the moon."

3. Semicolons

Use a semicolon to separate a series of items if one or more of those items contains a comma.

My favorite gems are emeralds, which are green; sapphires, which are blue; and rubies, which are red.

4. Colons

Use a colon to introduce a list either after "these" or "the following" or in a place where "and here it is" or "and here they are" could be inserted. Do not use a colon right after a verb.

| CORRECT | These students won awards: Jaime, Mai, Malcolm, and Suzi. |
| INCORRECT | The winners were: Jaime, Mai, Malcolm, and Suzi. |

5. Dashes

Use a dash to show an abrupt break in thought or speech.

Hold your end up high—oh, you dropped it!

6. Hyphens

6.1 Use a hyphen to link words in some compound words. If you have doubts about whether to use a hyphen in a compound, look up the compound in a dictionary.

HYPHENATED COMPOUNDS

all-powerful queen
twentieth-century history
well-known musician
middle-class person
self-confident speaker
living-room furniture
blue-green color
problem-solving ability
five-year-old boy
great-grandson

6.2 Use a hyphen to separate numbers.

2005-2006 school year

pp. 21-43 and 183-85

7. Parentheses

Use parentheses to set off added information that is not part of the main idea of the sentence.

Tomorrow (my birthday) we will be seeing a film called *Donald Duck in Mathmagic Land.*

8. Apostrophes

8.1 For most nouns and some, but not all, pronouns, use an apostrophe to show ownership or belonging.

For a singular noun, add an apostrophe and an *s.*

an eagle's eye

the moon's dark side

To show ownership or possession for a plural noun, add only an apostrophe if the plural noun ends in *s.* Add an apostrophe and an *s* if the plural noun ends in some letter other than *s.*

the workers' lunchboxes

the children's choir

More ▶

To show ownership or belonging by all members of a group, use the apostrophe only for the last one in the group.

> **This is Tom, Carla, and Marshall's house.**

8.2 To show belonging, use an apostrophe with a word that refers to a time or to an amount of currency or coin.

> **a year's time**
>
> **a nickel's worth of duck food**

8.3 Use an apostrophe to form contractions.

> **'80s music, 12 o'clock, don't**

9. Italics and Underlining

9.1 Use italics (when word processing) or underlining (when writing longhand) for titles of

works of art: Leonardo da Vinci's *Mona Lisa*

books: J. R. R. Tolkien's *Return of the King*

plays: *You're a Good Man, Charlie Brown*

films: *Star Wars: The Phantom Menace*

television series: *Sesame Street*

magazines: *Cricket, Highlights, Ranger Rick*

long musical works such as operas: the *Nutcracker Ballet, Peter and the Wolf*

Do not use italics or underlining for names of musical forms such as concertos or symphonies.

> **Beethoven's Symphony no. 5**

9.2 Use italics (when word processing) or underlining (when writing longhand) for words used as words, letters used as letters, and words from foreign languages.

> **The vowels are *a, e, i, o,* and *u*.**
>
> **The name *Bob*, spelled backward, is the name *Bob*.**
>
> **The Sanskrit word *padme* means "lotus."**
>
> **"*Lo siento*," said Miguel.**

10. Quotation Marks

10.1 Use quotation marks to enclose direct quotations but not indirect quotations.

USE QUOTES   Pablo Picasso said, "Every child is an artist."

DO NOT USE QUOTES   Did Picasso say that all children are artists?

10.2 Commas or periods after a quotation should go inside the closing quotation marks.

"Let a smile be your umbrella," I always say.

10.3 Colons and semicolons should go outside the quotation marks.

I said, "Good morning, Mr. Scrooge"; however, he just ignored me.

Mark said this about "The Trouble with Tribbles": "It is the best *Star Trek* episode ever made."

10.4 A question mark should go inside the quotation marks if the quoted material is a question. Otherwise, the question mark should go outside the quotation marks.

Did the alien say, "Take me to your leader"?

Did the alien ask, "Who is your leader?"

11. Ellipses

11.1 Use an **ellipsis** (…) to show that material has been left out.

"No sensible decision can be made … without taking into account the world as it will be."   —Isaac Asimov

11.2 Use an ellipsis to show a pause in dialogue, or speech that is unfinished.

"Hey, … wait for me," said Hector.

"This is really, really…." Ms. Nogales stopped, too choked up to finish her thank-you's.

12. Capitalization
12.1

Capitalize the first letter in each main word in the following:	Example
The names of historical events	the Battle of Shiloh
Special events	the Watermelon Seed-Spitting Contest
Periods of time	the Roaring Twenties; the Ice Age
Interjections used alone	Oh! Well! I never!
Brand names	Converse, Gap
Letters used as grades	two As and three Bs on my report card
Musical tones	an E-flat scale
Names of organizations and institutions	The Academy of Motion Picture Arts and Sciences
Personal names	John Jones
Place names	Ocala, Florida
Proper nouns and adjectives	the Empire State Building; Hawaiian shirt
The pronoun *I*	me, myself, and I
Sacred names	Allah, Jehovah, Vishnu, Buddha, Mary, the Bible, the Koran
Course titles (as opposed to school subjects)	Fine Arts with Ms. Fleck
Vehicles	Air Force One; a Volkswagen Beetle
Months and days	Tuesday, April 1, 1943
Astronomical terms	Neptune, Orion
Works of art, literature, and music	*The Wind in the Willows;* "Happy Birthday"

More ▶

12.2 Capitalize the first letter in each important word in the names of family relationships used as titles except when these names are preceded by a modifier such as a personal pronoun.

> my dad
>
> Thank you, Father.
>
> Felicia's cousin
>
> my brother-in-law
>
> I say, Brother-in-Law dear, shall we depart?

12.3 Capitalize the first letter in each entry in an outline.

> Things to do
>
> > I. Get good grades
> >
> > II. Go to college
> >
> > III. Graduate with honors
> >
> > IV. Run for president

Appendix B:
"Student-Friendly" Writing Rubric[1]

Here is a six-point writing rubric that you can use to score essays that you write for this book. (A 6 is the highest score.)

6 Points	My ideas are interesting and well organized. My voice and feelings shine through. The writing is perfect for my purpose. My words are powerful, and my sentences are smooth. The writing follows correctly the conventions of grammar, usage, spelling, and mechanics.
5 Points	My ideas are on topic and their organization is easy to follow. The voice has energy and is just right for my purpose. My words and sentences are clear most of the time. I've checked the conventions and corrected the errors I know about.
4 Points	I have a main idea but could use better-organized details. The voice sounds like me in parts and is OK for my purpose. I could use some more exact words and smooth some of the sentences. I need to correct a few errors in conventions.
3 Points	My ideas are a little unclear, and their organization is hard to follow. I'm not sure if the voice sounds like me or fits my purpose. I need to choose stronger words and smooth many choppy sentences. I can see lots of conventions errors. This needs editing.
2 Points	My main idea is hard to find, and the writing is not organized well. There's no life in the voice, and my purpose isn't clear. My words are dull, and my sentences have lots of problems. There are way too many errors in conventions.
1 Point	There's no main idea and no organization to what is here. I don't hear the right voice or see any purpose in this writing. My words and sentences are hard to understand. There are so many conventions errors that this is hard to read.

---

[1]This rubric is based upon the Write Traits™ writing program, published by Great Source Education Group, a division of Houghton Mifflin.

Glossary

Abbreviation. A shortened form of a word or name, such as Eng. for "England" or F.B.I. for "Federal Bureau of Investigation."

Abstract. General, not concrete or specific. *Happy, evil,* and *perfect* are abstract words.

Achievement test. A test that measures what a student has learned. Compare with *aptitude test.*

Active reading. Becoming involved with your reading by asking questions, visualizing, predicting, drawing conclusions, summarizing, evaluating, and making connections.

Active vocabulary. The vocabulary that you actually use; your speaking and writing vocabulary. Compare with *passive vocabulary.*

Active voice. Sentence in which the subject comes before the verb. *Dan washed the car* is in the active voice. Compare with *passive voice.*

Alliteration. Repeated consonant sounds at the beginnings of words, as in "Molly and Mary and Maggie and me."

Analysis. Breaking something down into its parts and studying each part to see what it does and how it relates to the whole.

Antonym. A word that is opposite or nearly opposite in meaning to another word. *Cold* and *hot* are antonyms. Compare with *synonym.*

Aptitude test. A test that tries to measure a person's underlying ability or potential. Compare with *achievement test.*

Arrangement. See *organization.*

Assonance. The use of identical vowel sounds in stressed syllables that have different consonant sounds, as in *black cat.*

Audience. The people for whom you are writing; your readers.

Author. Writer.

Autobiography. The true story of a person's life, or some part of the person's life, as told by that person. Compare with *biography.*

Base word. A complete word that is combined with one or more other word parts to make a new word. The base word *made* appears, for example, in the words *unmade* and *man-made.*

Biography. The true story of a person's life, or part of his or her life, as told by someone else. Compare with *autobiography.*

Body. In an essay, the main part of the piece of writing. The body appears after the introduction and before the conclusion. It presents ideas, examples, and other details to support the main idea, or thesis statement.

Boldface. Heavy, dark printing, like this: **This sentence is in boldface.**

Brainstorming. A technique for coming up with ideas. One or more people list as many ideas on a topic as possible, in as short a time as possible, without stopping to judge or think about any one idea.

Caption. Words next to or below a photo or illustration that tell about it. See *illustration.*

Cause. An event that brings about or helps to bring about another event. Compare with *effect.*

Cause-and-effect order. A type of organization in which causes are followed by effects or effects are followed by causes.

Character. A person or animal that takes part in the action of a story.

Chart. A graphic organizer with rows and columns for recording and displaying information. See *graphic organizer.*

Checklist. A list of items to be checked off as they are completed. See, for example, the Revision Checklist on page 196.

Chronological order. See *time order.*

Classroom test. A test given to measure what students in a class have learned.

Clause. A group of words that has a subject and a verb. See *dependent clause, independent clause.*

Clincher sentence. A sentence that summarizes or otherwise ends a paragraph. The clincher sentence appears at or near the end of a paragraph. Also called a *concluding sentence.*

Cluster chart. See *word web.*

Command. A type of sentence in which the speaker tells someone to do something.

Comparison. Showing the ways in which two or more things are alike. See also *contrast.*

Comparison-and-contrast order. A type of organization in which similarities are followed by differences or differences are followed by similarities.

Complex sentence. A sentence that contains one independent clause and one or more dependent clauses.

Compound-complex sentence. A sentence that contains more than one independent clause and one or more dependent clauses.

Compound sentence. A sentence that contains more than one independent clause and more than one complete thought.

Compound word. A word made up of two or more base words, as in *eightfold* or *breakdown.* Compounds can be solid (one word), as in *spacecraft;* hyphenated, as in *space-time;* or open, as in *space shuttle.*

Comprehension. Understanding something. See *reading comprehension.*

Conclusion. The last part, or end, of a piece of writing. In fiction, the end of the story. In nonfiction, the final part in which the writer sums up the piece or ties his or her ideas together to make a point.

Conflict. A struggle or problem faced by a character.

Conjunction. In grammar, a word used to join two parts together. The coordinating conjunctions in English are *and, or, nor, for, but, so,* and *yet.*

Connecting. Thinking about the ways in which what you are reading relates to your own life. Connecting is an active reading strategy.

Connecting words. Words that show how ideas are related to one another. Examples include *for example, first, because,* and *therefore.* Also known as *transitions* or *transitional words and phrases.*

Context clue. In a piece of writing, words nearby that give information about the meaning of an unknown word.

Contrast. Showing the ways in which two or more things are different.

Conventions. The rules for using capital letters and punctuation marks. Some people also include in conventions the rules for manuscript form (indented paragraphs, margins, and so on).

Dangling modifier. A word or phrase that is supposed to be a modifier but appears in a sentence containing no word or phrase that the word or phrase can reasonably modify. The italicized phrase in this sentence is a dangling modifier: *After washing the car*, the real fun began.

Define. To explain the meaning of a word. You can do this by restating its meaning in other words that mean the same thing. You can also do it by giving examples.

Degree order. A type of organization in which ideas or information is presented from more to less or from less to more. An example of degree order is organization by importance (from least important to most important, or the reverse).

Dependent clause, or subordinate clause. A group of words that has a subject and a verb but cannot stand alone as a sentence. Compare with *independent clause*.

Describe. To show, in writing or in speech, how something looks, feels, smells, tastes, or sounds.

Descriptive writing. Writing that uses words to set a scene or create a portrait of a subject.

Detail. An example or other specific piece of information. A fact about a person, place, or idea would be a detail.

Diary. See *journal*.

Directions. Step-by-step instructions telling how to do something.

Drafting. The part of the writing process in which you get your ideas down on paper, but not in final form.

Effect. A result. One or more events that happen because of one or more other events. Compare with *cause*.

Elaboration. 1. Providing additional ideas or information to support an idea, point of view, or description. Writers elaborate by including specific details, examples, facts, opinions, paraphrases, quotations, reasons, and summaries. 2. In a paragraph, any statement that supports a topic sentence or thesis statement. See *supporting details, thesis*.

Ellipsis. Three or four dots (...) used to show that material is missing from a quotation. An ellipsis can also indicate a pause in a character's speech.

Essay. A piece of nonfiction writing that is more than one paragraph long and explores a single part of a larger topic.

Evaluating. Studying whether something is good or bad, right or wrong, strong or weak; forming an opinion about the qualities of something.

Event. Something that happens.

Evidence. Information given to prove or support a general statement or opinion.

Example. Something selected to show the nature or character of the rest of a group; a typical instance. Examples are often used as context clues and as a type of supporting detail. See *elaboration*.

Exclamation. A sentence that expresses strong feeling and ends with an exclamation point (!).

Exclamation mark. A punctuation mark (!) used to end a sentence that expresses strong feeling.

Explain. Give reasons, causes, or details to tell how or why.

Expository writing. Writing that presents information. Also known as *informative writing*.

Expressive writing. Writing that is mostly about the writer's personal thoughts and feelings.

Extended-response question. A question that asks you to come up with an answer that is usually longer than a paragraph. You may have to support your answer with specific facts and examples from something you have just read.

Fable. A short tale with animal characters that is told to teach a moral, or lesson. See also *moral, parable.*

Fact. A statement that can be proved to be true. A fact is true by definition or can be proved by observation. Compare with *opinion.*

Fiction. A story about imaginary characters and events. Compare with *nonfiction.*

Figure of speech. Descriptive language that is not meant to be taken literally, including *personifications, similes,* and *metaphors.*

Final draft. A final version of a piece of writing—one that has been revised and, usually, proofread.

Five-paragraph theme. See *standard classroom theme.*

Focused. Related to the topic. A piece of writing is focused if it does not wander onto unrelated topics.

Folktale. A story that originated in the oral tradition and that has been passed down by word of mouth from one generation to the next.

Form. The shape that your writing will take. For example, it might be a letter, a paragraph, or an essay.

Fragment. A group of words that does not express a complete idea and so is not a complete sentence. Often, the subject or the verb is missing.

Freewriting. Coming up with ideas by simply writing whatever comes into your head about a topic. When you freewrite, you put down any and all ideas and do not stop to worry about correctness.

Function. What something does; its purpose.

Genre. A form or type of written work, such as a letter, a persuasive essay, or a novel.

Grammar. The rules that tell how words and word parts can be combined into phrases and sentences.

Graphic organizer. A chart, outline, or drawing used to present or organize ideas. Graphic organizers can be used for notetaking as well as prewriting (planning what you will say and how you will say it).

Heading. A subhead (or section title) that appears within a reading selection.

History. 1. The study of the past. 2. A true story about the past.

Illustration. A picture, drawing, or map.

Imperative sentence. A sentence that gives a command or makes a request.

Implied. Hinted at, but not directly stated.

Independent clause. A group of words that has a subject and a verb and that can stand alone as a sentence.

Informative writing. Writing that presents facts, not opinions. See also *expository writing.*

Integration. Keeping it together; explaining or expressing ideas in such a way that they hang together, flow smoothly, and make sense.

Interrogative sentence. A sentence that asks a question and that ends with a question mark (?).

Introduction. The beginning part of a long piece of writing. The introduction usually tells the main idea.

Italics. Slanted type, like this: *This sentence is in italics.*

Journal. A day-by-day telling in writing of your thoughts, of events in your life, or of anything else that you want to write about. Also called a *diary.*

Key words. The most important words in a selection.

Lead. The opening line in a piece of writing. Writers usually try to make the lead interesting to grab the attention of readers. A lead might ask a question, quote someone, tell a story, or give an interesting fact.

Leader line. In a multiple-choice question, the part that comes before the answers. Sometimes the leader line is a question. Sometimes it contains a blank to be filled in. Sometimes it is a sentence to be completed by the correct answer.

Learning log. A journal in which you record what you have learned.

Listing. Jotting down a number of items.

Logical organization. The arrangement of ideas in a piece of writing in an order that makes sense. See also *organization.*

Main idea. The central idea that a piece of writing or speech is mostly about, or one or more important ideas in a speech or piece of writing.

Making connections. Thinking about what one thing has to do with another or how it affects something else. Making connections is an active reading strategy. Good readers connect what they read to what they already know.

Manuscript form. The layout of a piece of writing on a page. Manuscript form includes the type of spacing, margin width, indention of paragraphs, and the placement of titles, captions, headings, page numbers, and the writer's name. For student papers, manuscript form usually includes the writer's class and teacher, as well as the date.

Mechanics. Punctuation and capitalization.

Metaphor. A figure of speech in which one thing is described as if it were another, as in *Paul Bunyan, that mountain of a man.*

Misplaced modifier. A word or phrase placed in a sentence in such a way that it modifies the wrong word or phrase. The italicized phrase in this sentence is a misplaced modifier: *Taking pictures with their digital cameras,* the monkeys gave the tourists quite a treat.

Modifier. Grammatical term referring to a word, phrase, or clause that limits (by making more specific) the meaning of another word, phrase, or clause. Adjectives, adverbs, adjective phrases, adverb phrases, and other parts of speech that perform the functions of these are examples of modifiers. In the phrase *a good book, good* is a modifier of *book.*

Mood. The emotional quality created by a piece of writing. Joy, fear, sadness, and suspense are all examples of mood.

Moral. A type of theme that tells how people should or should not think or act; a lesson. See also *fable, parable*.

Motive. That which leads a character to think, feel, or act in a certain way.

Multiple-choice question. A question that gives several possible answers from which to choose the correct answer.

Narrative. A story, either fiction or nonfiction.

Narrative nonfiction. A true story.

Narrative writing. Writing that tells a story.

Narrator. The voice that tells a story.

Narrowing a topic. Making a topic more specific, or less general. For example, the topic "*Star Wars, Episode I*" is more narrow than the topic "science-fiction and fantasy movies."

Nonfiction. Writing about real people, places, things, or ideas. Compare with *fiction*.

Notes. A shorthand written record or reminder about something.

Novel. A long piece of narrative fiction.

Objective. Presenting only facts and not personal opinions. News reports, for example, are supposed to be objective.

Onomatopoeia. Words or groups of words, like *buzz* or *meow*, that sound like what they describe.

Open-ended question. A type of question for which you must come up with and write out your own answer, often at some length.

Opinion. A statement that cannot be proved, absolutely, to be true or false. Compare with *fact*.

Oral tradition. Songs, stories, and poems passed down by word of mouth, especially before people used writing.

Organization. The method of arrangement of ideas in a piece of writing. For example, a writer might organize her ideas in time order or in spatial order. See also *logical organization*.

Outline. See *rough outline*.

Parable. A short tale with human characters that is told to teach a moral, or lesson. See also *fable, moral*.

Paragraph. A unit of writing, usually with more than one sentence, that gets across a main idea. A *paragraph in standard form* is a unit of writing with a topic sentence, two or more supporting sentences, and, often, a concluding or clincher sentence.

Parallelism. The use of similar grammatical forms to give sentence parts equal weight, as in Abraham Lincoln's "of the people, by the people, for the people."

Paraphrase. 1. (*v.*) To repeat in different words an idea taken from another speaker or writer. 2. (*n.*) A piece of speech or writing that repeats, in different words, an idea taken from another speaker or writer.

Passive vocabulary. The vocabulary that you understand but do not use in your own writing or speech. Compare with *active vocabulary*.

Persuasion. Writing or speech that tries to get the audience to do or believe something.

Persuasive writing. Writing that tries to get the reader to agree with the writer's point of view. The writer often urges the reader to change his or her beliefs or to take some action.

Phrase. A group of words that does not contain a subject and a verb, such as *in the sky* or *the big, blue whale.*

Plot. The series of events in a story.

Poetry. Language used in a special way to get across ideas or feelings. Poetry is often written in verse with a regular rhythm.

Predicate. The part of a sentence that is not the subject, including the verb and any words that modify or complete the verb. Compare with *subject.* See also *verb phrase.*

Predicting. Guessing what will happen in the future. Predicting what will happen in a narrative is an active reading strategy.

Prefix. A word part, such as *de-*, *in-*, or *mono-*, added to the beginning of a word or word part, as in *de- + value = devalue.*

Prereading. See *previewing.*

Prereading questions. Ones you make up before you read the whole text. Questions that you expect to be answered when you read the text carefully.

Previewing. Activities that a reader does before reading a selection, including scanning for parts like the title and key words, thinking about the topic, and asking questions. Also called *prereading.*

Prewriting. Part of the writing process in which you choose a topic, gather ideas, and organize your ideas.

Prior knowledge. What you already know about a subject.

Process. Anything that takes place over time and that involves change. A process usually involves a series of steps.

Process essay. An essay that gives directions or explains the steps in a process.

Process of writing. All the steps that a writer takes when creating a piece of writing. Major steps in the process of writing include prewriting, drafting, evaluating and revising, proofreading, and publishing.

Proofreading. Looking over a piece of writing to find and correct errors in spelling, grammar, usage, punctuation, and capitalization.

Prose. Writing that is organized into sentences and paragraphs rather than into lines of verse, as in poetry.

Publishing. Sharing your writing with others. You can do this, for example, by handing out copies to friends, by sending it in an e-mail, or by reading it aloud.

Purpose. What a writer wants his or her writing to do. For example, a writer's purpose might be to inform or to entertain.

Questioning. Asking about something. A question often begins with *who, what, where, when, why,* or *how.* Questioning is an active reading strategy.

Quotation. The exact words of another speaker or writer, repeated verbatim (word for word).

Reading comprehension. Understanding the main points of a piece of writing or what happens in a story. The process of making meaning from a piece of writing.

Reasonable opinion. An opinion that is supported by facts and reflects good values.

Recording. Taking notes on what you are hearing, seeing, or reading.

Reference work. A source of information that is reliable, such as a dictionary, almanac, encyclopedia, atlas, or database.

Reflecting. Thinking about what you have read, heard, or seen.

Responding. Thinking about and doing something active in reaction to what you are hearing, seeing, or reading.

Revising. Making changes to improve a piece of writing. For example, you might revise to make the content more interesting. You also might revise to make the organization clearer.

Rhyme. The repetition of sounds at the ends of words, as in *elevator* and *traitor*.

Rhyme scheme. The pattern of rhymes in a poem.

Rhythm. The pattern of strong and weak beats in a poem.

Root. A basic word part that gives the main meaning of a word even though it cannot stand alone as a word. Examples of roots include *capt* in *captive* and *capture*, and *dem* in *democracy* and *democrat*.

Rough draft. An early, unfinished version of a piece of writing. Compare with *final draft*.

Rough outline. A quick outline containing main ideas and supporting ideas that are written beneath the main ideas. Supporting ideas are usually introduced by dashes (—).

Rubric. A list of guidelines or scoring criteria for a piece of writing (or other work project).

Run-on. Two separate sentences incorrectly run together and treated as one.

Scanning. Looking through a piece of writing quickly to find specific parts or information.

Sentence. A group of words that has a subject and a verb and that tells a complete idea.

Sentence combining. The act of putting separate sentences together into a single sentence.

Sentence expanding. Revision of a sentence by adding words, phrases, or clauses.

Sentence fragment. See *fragment*.

Sentence frame. A simple sentence to which parts can be added to make more complicated sentences.

Sequence. The order in which things happen in a piece of writing.

Setting. The time and place in which a story happens.

Simile. A type of metaphor that makes a comparison using *like, as,* or *than*, as in "Spring came like a freight train, fast and furious." Compare with *metaphor*.

Simple sentence. A sentence that has only one subject/verb pair, as in *Maria swims often*. The subject and verb may be compound, as in *Jack and Jill tripped and fell*.

Short-response question. A question that asks you to write a short answer (a few sentences to a paragraph in length) or fill in a chart.

Skimming. Previewing a piece of writing by looking it over quickly to get a general idea about its content.

Spatial order. In order of location, such as from left to right or from top to bottom.

Standard classroom theme. An essay that contains an introductory paragraph, two or three body paragraphs that support the thesis (main idea) given in the introductory paragraph, and a concluding paragraph.

Statement. A sentence that tells something about a person, place, or thing. It ends with a period.

Stringy sentence. A sentence that contains many parts loosely combined with conjunctions such as *and* or *but*. See also *run-on*.

Structure. How something is organized or put together.

Style. The qualities of a piece of writing that make it unique. See also *voice*.

Subhead. See *heading*.

Subject. 1. What a piece of writing is about. 2. In a sentence, the doer of the action of the verb. Compare with *predicate*.

Subordinate clause. See *dependent clause*.

Suffix. A word part, such as *-al*, *-ment*, or *-tion*, added to the end of a word or word part, as in *merry + -ment = merriment*.

Summarize. To say again or tell what happened in fewer and different words. Summarizing is an active reading strategy.

Summary. A piece of speech or writing that repeats an idea or group of ideas in different and fewer words.

Supporting detail. A fact, opinion, example, or other kind of detail that explains or illustrates a main idea. See also *detail, elaboration*.

Supporting sentences. In a paragraph, the sentences that support, or give more information about, the topic sentence.

Symbol. 1. Something that stands for another thing besides itself. A rose is a traditional symbol of love and beauty. 2. A special mark that stands for something beyond itself, such as a + for *and*.

Synonym. A word that has the same or a similar meaning to another word. *Huge* and *massive* are synonyms. Compare with *antonym*.

Theme. A main idea, lesson, or moral. In a story, the theme is sometimes a lesson that the main character learns.

Thesis. In a long piece of writing such as an essay, a one- or two-sentence statement of the main idea. Also called the *thesis statement*.

Thesis statement. See *thesis*.

Time order. The order in which something happens. Same as *chronological order*.

Title. The name of a piece of writing. The title usually appears at the beginning of the piece.

Tone. The attitude of a narrator or a character.

Topic sentence. In a paragraph, a sentence that tells the main idea.

Transition. See *transitional words and phrases*.

Transitional words and phrases. Words and phrases, such as *after, then, next, as a result, in summary*, and *therefore*, used to show connections between or among ideas. See *connecting words*.

Underlining. Placing a line under one or more letters or words: <u>This sentence is underlined.</u>

Verb. A word or phrase that names an action, such as *run* or *has been sleeping;* or a word or phrase like *is* or *will be* that describes a state of being.

Verb phrase. A group of words containing a verb and its modifiers (words that describe or tell about it) and complements (such as direct or indirect objects).

Visualizing. Picturing something in your head. Visualizing is an active reading strategy.

Vocabulary. 1. All the words a person or group of people knows. 2. A list of words, particularly of new or unfamiliar words from a reading passage.

Voice. The unique sound of a piece of writing. Voice is created by a writer's style. See *style*.

Word web. A type of graphic organizer that you make this way: Write down an idea and circle it. Write related ideas around the first idea. Circle these and draw lines to connect them to the first idea. Continue in this way until you have enough ideas. Also called a *cluster chart*.

Wordiness. The use of many words when fewer will do.

Writing prompt. A short set of directions or instructions for doing a piece of writing.

Written-response question. A questions that requires you to write your answer (as opposed to providing answers from which to choose). See *short-response question* and *extended-response question*.

Index

A
abbreviation, 155
action words, 182
active listening, 166–168
active reading strategies, 65–86
alliteration, 142
answers, 44; how to write, 203
apostrophes, 277–278
assonance, 139
audience, 183
author, 65, 167
autobiography, 129

B
base word, 77
biography, 129
body (of an essay), 229, 234–235

C
capitalization, 280–281
captions, 65
cause(s), 87, 96–97, 108, 123, 125
cause-and-effect order, 123
characters, 130, 134, 135, 167
chart(s), 160
chronological (time) order, 123, 189
clause, 275; independent, 276
clincher (concluding) sentence, 222
cluster chart, 159, 186
colons, 276
command, 208

commas, 275–276
comparing, 125, 182
comparison, 76, 80
comparison-and-contrast order, 123
compound predicate, 215
compound sentence, 214
compound word, 77
concluding sentence, 222
conclusion, 65, 229, 236
conflict, 134, 135
conjunctions, 214; coordinating, 215
connecting, 70, 166
connections, making, 70
context, 100–101, 108; clues, 75–76, 100, 108
contrasting, 76, 125, 182
coordinating conjunctions, 215
correcting, 203

D
dashes, 276
defining, 182
degree order, 123
describing, 182
descriptive writing, 118
detail(s), 154, 168; supporting, 222–225, 234–235
drafting, 180, 192–193, 203

E
effect(s), 87, 96–97, 108, 123, 125
ellipses, 279
end marks, 275

essay(s), 229–238; parts of, 229; process, 124
evaluating, 85, 180, 195–197, 203
events, 93, 130, 167
example, 75
exclamation, 208
explaining, 182
extended-response question(s), 54

F
fable, 105, 135
fact(s), 119
fiction, 134–146, 167; features of, 134
form, 183
fragment, 205
freewriting, 186

G
gathering information, 186
graphic organizer(s), 159; chart, 160; cluster chart, 186; timeline, 161; Venn diagram, 162; word web, 159, 186

H
headings, 65
history, 129
hyphens, 277

I
illustrations, 65
implied subject, 208
independent clause, 276
inference, 76
informative, nonfiction, 124; writing, 118

introduction, 65, 229, 231–233
italics, 278

K
key words, 65, 108

L
lead, 232–233
leader line, 44
listening, 166–174
listing, 186

M
main idea(s), 87, 88–89, 108, 168, 184, 222–228
moral, 105
multiple-choice question(s), 44–45, 54; how to answer, 45

N
narrative(s), 167; writing, 118
narrative nonfiction, 118, 129–130; features of, 130; types of, 129
New York ELA exam, 53–56
nonfiction, 116–133, 167, 168; features of, 117; narrative, 129–130; tips for reading, 133
notetaking, 152–174; symbols and abbreviations, 155; tips, 152, 155

O
onomatopoeia, 142
opinion(s), 47, 119
order, cause-and-effect, 123; chronological (time), 123, 189; comparison-and-contrast, 123; degree, 123; of importance, 189; spatial, 123, 189
organization, 117; methods of, 123
outline. *See* rough outline.

P
paragraph, 222–228
parentheses, 277
parenthetical expression, 275
persuasive writing, 118
phrase(s), 154, 214; verb, 205, 214
plot, 134, 167
poetry, 138–146
predicate, 205, 214; compound, 215
predicting, 69, 166
prefix, 77, 78
prereading questions, 65, 85
previewing, 65
prewriting, 180–190, 203
process, 179
process essay, 124
proofreading, 180, 199, 203
proofreading checklist, 199
publishing, 180, 203
purpose, 117, 118, 182

Q
question(s), 207
questioning, 69, 166
quotation marks, 279

R
reading comprehension, 87–108
reading strategies review, 108

reflecting, 85
responding, 85–89
restatement, 75
revision, 180, 195; checklist, 196; symbols, 200
rhyme, 139; scheme, 139
rhythm, 138–139
root, 77, 80–81
rough outline, 189, 234
run-on, 217

S
scanning, 65, 108
semicolons, 276
sentence(s), clincher, 222; combining, 213; complete, 205; compound, 214; concluding, 222; fragment(s), 205; simple, 213; supporting, 223; topic, 222; types, 207–210
sequence, 87, 93, 108; clues, 93
setting, 130, 134, 135, 167
short-response question(s), 54
simple sentences, 213
spatial order, 123, 189
standardized test(s), how to approach, 51
standards, 53
statement, 207; thesis, 117, 231
story, 167
subheads, 65
subject, 117, 168, 205; implied, 208
suffix, 77, 79–80
summarizing, 70, 166, 182

supporting details, 168, 222–225, 234–235
supporting sentences, 223
symbol, 155

T

test(s), how to approach, 51; standardized, 51
test questions, 44–47
theme, 87, 104, 108, 130, 134, 135, 145, 167; questions, 105
thesis, 117, 229, 231
thesis statement, 117, 231, 233
timeline, 161
title, 65, 167
topic, 182; choosing, 184; narrowing, 184
topic sentence, 222, 234
transitions (words that connect ideas), 223

U

underlining, 278

V

Venn diagram, 162
verb, 205
verb phrase, 205, 214
visualizing, 69, 166
vocabulary, 87

W

word(s), base, 77; compound, 77; that connect ideas, 223
word family, 77, 80–81
word parts, 77–78, 100
word web, 159, 186
writing, 175–204; descriptive, 118; evaluating and revising, 195–197, 203; informative, 118; narrative, 118; persuasive, 118; process, 179–204; types of, 118. *See also* freewriting; prewriting.
writing prompt, 181, 231
written-response question(s), 46–47